KILLER INSTINCT

HAVING A MIND FOR MURDER

DONALD GRANT

MELBOURNE
UNIVERSITY
PRESS

MELBOURNE UNIVERSITY PRESS
An imprint of Melbourne University Publishing Limited
Level 1, 715 Swanston Street, Carlton, Victoria 3053, Australia
mup-contact@unimelb.edu.au
www.mup.com.au

First published 2018
Text © Donald A Grant, 2018
Design and typography © Melbourne University Publishing Limited, 2018

Cover design by Philip Campbell Design
Typeset by Megan Ellis
Printed in Australia by McPherson's Printing Group

A catalogue record for this
book is available from the
National Library of Australia

ISBN 9780522873597 (paperback)
ISBN 9780522873603 (ebook)

PRAISE FOR *KILLER INSTINCT*

It is a terrifying insight into the killer within. By laying bare the crimes, compulsions and twisting contradictions of ten individual killers, Grant succeeds in exposing something even more disturbing—that each of us is capable, at our worst, of something dark and violent. In a lifetime spent working with hundreds of murderers and thousands more who have committed brutal acts, Grant has learned to strip away their defences, revealing the base instincts, bitter childhoods and self-serving justifications that led them to commit the very worst of crimes. He has attempted to inhabit the minds of these murderers and to understand their actions. The result—this book—is painful, honest and unflinching. More compelling than any crime fiction, *Killer Instinct* should be required reading, for it reveals how the line between good and evil lies very close to home.

Dan Box, host of the *Bowraville* podcast series, winner of two Walkley awards and the Sir Keith Murdoch and Les Kennedy awards

Killer Instinct … is an intriguing read. It gives a fascinating insight into the world of killers, forensic psychiatry and the legal system, including the difficulties of predicting dangerousness.

Who hasn't wondered if, given a particular set of circumstances or mental illness, they might be driven to kill another?

Forensic psychiatrist Donald Grant, whose reports I read with confidence during my twenty-six years as a judge, explores that and other big questions, such as who is capable of rehabilitation, who has rehabilitated, and who is beyond redemption.

Margaret McMurdo, immediate past President, Court of Appeal, Queensland Supreme Court

What a great book! A fascinating and compelling read. From the outset, you are struck by the authenticity of the authorial voice. Donald Grant is not some sensationalist hack looking to beat up a story for cheap thrills. This is a book by a trained professional intimately involved in the affairs described. Over the course of his career, he has seen a lot. There is tremendous variety in the case studies. Each is completely engrossing in its own particular way … You learn a lot from this text. It is perfectly paced with moments of reflection and diagnosis amidst the horror of sadism and murder.

Alastair Blanshard, Head of the School of Historical and Philosophical Enquiry, University of Queensland

This is a fascinating insight from one of Australia's leading forensic psychiatrists into an area of human behaviour that forever baffles most people. A must read for all of those interested, or involved in, cases of murder as to how the forensic psychiatrist unravels and makes sense of this often alarming and incomprehensible behaviour.

Fiona Judd, Professorial Fellow, Department of Psychiatry, University of Melbourne

Murder to most lay people, law enforcement officers and juries presents a real challenge in understanding the motivation behind such a heinous act. Utilising his forensic psychiatry skills, Dr Grant provides a very readable and compelling analysis of cases in which he has been involved, and should provide readers with a greater understanding of the psychological and psychiatric issues in the 'mad' versus 'bad' dichotomy.

Julian Davis, forensic psychiatrist

To all of my psychiatrist colleagues and friends who share with me the passion and challenges of this work, and whose support, camaraderie and peer review over many years have kept me reasonably sane and on track.

CONTENTS

AUTHOR'S NOTE

Murder has a high profile in the public psyche. The television and print media and films are full of murder stories. The most vicious or terrifying cases are reported in depth, sometimes with graphic images, maps and diagrams. Our curiosity seems insatiable: appalled by the tragedy, we're nonetheless attracted to every sordid detail. We speculate endlessly about the motivation of the murderer—second-guessing, becoming sleuths in coffee conversations. The subject of murder has become as safe as the weather, though much more fascinating.

Yet murder is a rare event. In Australia, the incidence of murder—the number of new cases per year—is very low, around one for every 100 000 people. In fact, in our society it is slowly reducing in frequency, possibly because of factors such as gun control and an improved understanding and treatment of mental health issues. In other societies the incidence of murder is much higher, for a range of social and cultural reasons.

Within Australia, the incidence of murder varies considerably across different sectors of society. The most common offenders are men aged twenty-five to forty-five. Murder occurs more frequently in cities than in rural locations, and has strong associations with domestic violence, alcohol and drug abuse, general criminality, gang activity, social instability and sometimes ethnicity. Two-thirds of murders occur in the home and the commonest weapon is a knife. Three-quarters of offenders are caught and charged within a short time.

As a young psychiatrist I became interested from a clinical perspective in the reasons why people become violent. Increasingly, over many years, I was drawn into the practice of forensic psychiatry, the criminal area of which involves the examination and assessment of people who have fallen foul of the law. Forensic psychiatrists come to this fascinating field from a background of medical qualification, experience in general medicine and then years of training in psychiatry, followed by clinical work honing interviewing and diagnostic skills and gaining expertise in treating patients with a wide variety of disorders. Good clinical skills are a vital prerequisite to a successful forensic career. To that basis must then be added specific training and treatment experience with forensic patients and developing a basic knowledge of the areas of law relevant to your assessments. Some of my forensic colleagues practise mainly in civil law areas, perhaps assessing accident victims claiming compensation or working in family court matters. While I have done many civil law assessments, in recent years my focus has been almost entirely on the criminal area, by which I am fascinated. Over the course of more than four decades of practice, I have assessed thousands of violent and sexual offenders. I estimate that I have reported upon more than 200 people who were charged with murder.

In this book I will tell you about ten of those murderers, all of them from Queensland. The great bulk of my medico-legal practice has taken place in that state and therefore been under the umbrella of its *Criminal Code* and *Mental Health Act*, which provides for a unique Mental Health Court. I am now writing about the minds of murderers not to cater to the endless fascination of the community but to explain the complexity of acts of murder and the nature of people who murder. Cultural contexts, social issues, personality factors, brain damage, mental illness and intoxication all have their place in the discussion; so too the processes of legal decision-making to which a forensic psychiatrist contributes through medico-legal assessment and evidence in court. The issues I address in presenting these murders include unsoundness of mind (referred to in other jurisdictions by alternative terms, such as impairment or insanity), diminished responsibility, intoxication, fitness for trial, and risk assessment. These and terms like them will be talked about to the extent necessary to make sense of the outcomes.

Many readers will not be familiar with the role of a forensic psychiatrist. I do not rush out to crime scenes, as forensic fiction would have you believe, nor do I gather evidence or assist police in finding the culprit. I do not attend autopsies, and I do not get involved in profiling possible offenders. I may be called upon after a charge is laid to assess the alleged offender, either soon after the murder or much later, before a trial. I am concerned not with *who did it*, but with *why they did it*.

I will be asked to prepare a report to assist the court in understanding the relevant clinical issues. I will then review all of the evidence and interview the offender at length—either in prison or in my rooms—in order to prepare my written opinion. In Queensland, this is distributed to the defence and prosecution counsels well before the trial, when I will be available for cross-examination. My role stops there—I give my opinion, and it is up to the court to weigh all the evidence and make its decision. I may comment on safety and treatment needs if the defendant were to be given a custodial sentence or detained in a psychiatric hospital, but I have no role in sentencing decisions.

To be able to tease out the motivations for a murder, it is necessary to look closely at the killing and the entire context in which it has occurred. The case examples in this book, drawn from the many murderers I have assessed, illustrate the unique circumstances that bring a person to murder—there are many kinds of murder and a wide variety of causes. A forensic psychiatrist must elicit great detail to get the full picture necessary to make a diagnosis, understand future risk and discern treatment for the offender. I have done this so many times and heard so many awful stories that I have developed the ability to generally maintain objectivity and not become too emotionally involved. Even so, some cases can creep under the barriers. For those who are not so familiar with explicit descriptions of violent and sexual offending, the subject matter of these cases may be very difficult to confront. But that detail is vital in coming to an accurate understanding of motivation that can lead to the correct assessment.

If there is such a thing as a common or garden-variety murderer, I am less likely to have been asked to assess them, as their offences will have obvious motivations that don't require psychiatric investigation. I am not generally asked to assess gangland assassinations or drug-world killings. Mass killers and terrorists may well be worthy of psychiatric attention, but I have never been involved with such accused. I am therefore not putting my case examples forward as a study of murderers from A to Z, but rather to illustrate more complex offenders, where there is possible interplay among issues such as relationship problems, personality disorder, intellectual handicap, mental illness and alcohol or drug abuse.

The ten cases in this book were chosen because they are all unusual in their own way. I found them challenging, intriguing and clinically fascinating in their particular details. I have tried to provide a range of ages and motivations to illustrate that murder does not just involve young antisocial men, jealous lovers or drug abusers but can touch almost anyone, given the critical mix of causal factors.

Using real cases raises important and delicate issues with regard to confidentiality and carries the risk of causing distress to victims' families, the offenders themselves and the communities where the offences occurred. I have given a lot of thought to these issues. I have named offenders and their victims because they are already in the public domain; where I refer to other family members or witnesses, I have changed the names to protect privacy.

Information about these offences is readily available on the public record. Court proceedings, evidence and findings are published and accessible on the internet. Many of the murders have also been extensively reported in the media, including coverage of the trials. Communities have been well acquainted with events in their locality. These matters are therefore not confidential. They may have dropped out of sight and, inevitably, discussing them again may be upsetting, but I hope all involved will understand that I have written about 'their' cases to further our understanding of why these shocking events occur, and also why some offenders are convicted of murder while others are given a psychiatric defence.

Sometimes, real cases are stranger than fiction, and they convey an authenticity that made-up examples would lack. It is precisely because they are real that they are of such value.

It is important to note that none of these cases were treatment patients under my care at any stage. If they were, medical confidentiality would apply and no sharing of information would be possible.

All the people I see for medico-legal assessments are made aware that the information they provide is not confidential, that it will go into my report and will then likely be available to all parties in open court proceedings. When I provide court reports, I am obliged to work within the *Code of Conduct for Expert Witnesses*, which stipulates that my responsibilities are to the court rather than to any of the separate parties. Whether the request comes from the prosecution, the defence or the court itself, I strive at all times to ensure my reports are impartial and independent.

The last section of this book is an appendix that explains the medico-legal maze offenders must navigate. The decision-making and disposition of offenders can be very difficult to understand and I hope this guide will provide clarity about the reasoning behind court decisions and assist with the accurate reporting of trial outcomes.

It has been a privilege to be given access to many people's lives and intimate experiences as part of my forensic psychiatric practice, and I offer those people my appreciation. My hope is that writing about these forensic cases will increase the understanding of the general public in regard to murder and murderers, and the legal processes that determine the mental capacities and future management of the offender.

OUR KILLER INSTINCT

Killer instinct. It's one of those phrases we might use from time to time to describe a characteristic of someone we know, usually a ruthless determination to come out on top in life. We don't mean literally that the person is going to kill someone. Yet, without knowing it, we may be making a rather profound statement about the origins of human aggression and the act of killing as a means of succeeding in life. I believe a primitive killer instinct still exists in all of us in some dormant form, controlled and civilised by our brain, our culture, our education, and our society's shared values and established rules of behaviour—an instinct capable of being released by powerful changes in our social or interpersonal life, or by developmental abnormalities or brain diseases. Any or all of these influences might effectively overcome our built-in controls and safeguards and release the primitive instinct to defend oneself, attack, and perhaps kill.

If such a latent killer instinct is part of our make-up, it is very well buried in most of us. But at the same time, we should be aware of the probability of a potential for aggression and violence, if not in ourselves, then in others around us. We speak of people we know who have a 'dark side' or a 'split personality' with a violent aspect to them. We hear of people who are very violent when intoxicated. We read and enjoy fictional accounts of Jekyll and Hyde, two opposing personas in the same man—one peaceful, the other aggressive—or tales of people who turn into vampires or werewolves, ready to kill. It seems we are aware at some level that there could be a killer instinct within us all.

This is frightening for most of us. We don't want to see ourselves in that light, no matter how buried and controlled such an instinct may be. We regard such a possibility as foreign and unacceptable. Any such thoughts of or indeed impulses towards violence are pushed well into our subconscious mind. For some of us, however, violent fantasies may hold a secret thrill or excitement, also generally kept in check by being banished from conscious enjoyment.

Could a suppressed killer instinct be the reason why so many of us are so morbidly fascinated by murder? We read every detail of murders that happen in our communities. We devour murder mystery novels. We watch an endless procession of television shows or films about real or fictional murder. We want to know who did it; we want the killer caught. Perhaps this fascination is one way of acknowledging our inner instinct and at the same time keeping it under control. By processing and controlling this external world of murder, we reassure ourselves that we can control the potential killer inside of us all.

Support for the notion of a killer instinct can be found in studies on the early development of humans as a species, observations of animal behaviour, and by comparing the brain of modern men and women with that of much earlier creatures from which we have evolved over millions of years.

Life from our evolutionary beginning was a matter of the survival of the fittest. The basic requirements to keep the species going had to be met: protecting your source of food and caring for yourself, your mate and your progeny. These in turn meant protecting your territory and getting rid of rivals. An instinct to kill was part of that defence system. But over time, indiscriminate killing didn't help the survival of any group of creatures. As evolution progressed, the use of lethal violence became more productively focused, used only against clear foreign threats. Within a given species, lesser degrees of aggression to settle contests for territory, or the right to mate with particular partners, became common. Rivals could show fierce but stylised aggressive displays that served the purpose of protecting their needs without actually risking killing off the species.

Over many millennia, this expression of the use of violence was modified and controlled by the development of extraordinary sophistication in the modern human brain, mirrored by cultural and societal structures and rules that dictated territorial and personal rights. Increasingly, violence and killing within a tribe or social group was deemed unacceptable, while still sanctioned against outsiders or other species. The primitive needs for food, territory and procreation continued to motivate conflicts and wars. The protection of one's own group or race remained a primal drive, and foreigners who looked different were a trigger for alarm and a likely violent attack, and killing. In some ways the human race hasn't changed all that much. Xenophobia and racism have ancient evolutionary origins.

Modern humans have evolved strong inhibitions against the killing of their own kind. The killer instinct has been reined in and suppressed in regard to fellow humans. It remains less suppressed when it comes to killing other species. The more distant and foreign a creature is from us, the easier it is to allow the killer instinct to be expressed. It is easier to kill a fly than a mouse, a mouse than a deer, a deer than a chimpanzee, that chimpanzee than a human. History shows that even within the human species, it has been easier to kill a fellow human if they are seen as subhuman, having a different colour, or even just having different religious practices. The ancient genetic conditioning to react to fear with potentially homicidal violence has proved very hard to completely civilise.

The changes that have evolved over millions of years to contain and control killing in human societies are reflected in us as individuals, right down to the make-up and function of our brains and minds. If you peel off the large hemispheres that distinguish the human brain from that of other species, you will find at its base structures that look and function like those of more primitive creatures. This part of our brain is sometimes referred to as our reptilian or crocodile brain. It comprises sensory organs that collect detailed information about what is happening around us, extensive memory stores that enable us to compare current happenings with past events, and the ready ability to spark alarm signals and arouse defensive and aggressive actions whenever a perceived threat appears. That part of our brain is, on its own, relatively uncontrolled and poorly discriminatory in making decisions to resort to violence. Primitive creatures that had only this reptilian brain saw no need for restraint.

As modern humans, we have evolved a huge frontal lobe to our brain, unique in the animal world. We have learned sophisticated means to harness aggression appropriately and to use it only in extreme circumstances. We have developed impulse control and intelligent decision-making that enable us to protect ourselves by alternative means and to think things through more sensibly. We have also developed the ability to generally work within the rules laid down by our cultural and legal systems. But the primitive part of our brain is still there and it still contains the basis for our killer instinct. That instinct can be released if our normal controls and inhibitions are degraded or removed by strong social influences: wartime propaganda that dehumanises our enemy; subcultural pressure from a gang or dissident group; interpersonal situations that threaten our most basic needs; physical disease or mental illness that disrupts our brain function and destroys our ability to reason; or intoxication with a substance that dissolves our inhibitions.

The killer instinct is therefore alive and well—dormant and out of conscious awareness for the most part, but nevertheless exerting some influence over our attitudes and behaviour. At some deep level we are aware of our potential for violence. Mostly, we are good at keeping that killer instinct on a tight leash. But our fear of the beast getting out of control lurks in the background of our minds. Our fascination with the murders committed by others is a reflection of the fear of our own inner murderous potential.

1

THE SMELL OF BLOOD

Forty-seven-year-old Edward Baldock sat naked on the grass on a cool October night in 1989. The popular Orleigh Park at West End was empty at midnight, the Brisbane River reflecting the lights of the city nearby. Edward's new acquaintance, Tracey, had just slipped off into the darkness to have a pee, having first taken off her shirt to reveal her breasts and offering to have sex when she came back. He had taken off his clothes, folded them in a pile, and pushed his wallet under the roller door of the rowing club a few metres away. He was fairly tipsy, having been out with mates at the Irish Club in Brisbane's CBD. He had walked across the river towards his inner-city home when Tracey and her friends called him over to their car and offered him a lift. He now sat waiting for what must have been an unexpected treat—sex with a woman twenty-five years his junior.

Sensing Tracey coming out of the darkness behind him, Edward said, 'What are you doing?' She replied, 'Nothing,' as she removed a knife from her trouser pocket. A second later, she plunged the knife up to its hilt in Edward's neck. He tried to grab her hand but she pushed his arm down. She withdrew the knife and stabbed him again, first in one side of the neck, then in the other. She continued stabbing him before grabbing his hair and slashing the knife across his throat. Despite his injuries, Edward was still alive. He made gurgling noises and rolled onto his side. Tracey again stabbed his neck, trying to get into the bones and cut the nerves. Blood welled from Edward's mouth. Tracey sat and watched him until, finally, he was motionless. To make sure he was dead, she plunged the knife deep into his side.

Tracey went to the river and threw in the knife, then washed her hands and arms. She dressed and returned to the car where her three friends had been waiting for the past half-hour. They were convinced Tracey was a vampire and that she had killed the man to drink his blood—she had earlier told them she 'needed to feed'. When she got back in the car, they were sure they could smell blood on her breath.

At 5 a.m. the following day, a jogger almost tripped over Edward's body. The naked man with gaping stab wounds and covered in blood was a sight no-one would want to see. Police were quickly summoned and a forensic pathologist was brought in to see the crime scene and examine the body. The main wounds were to the back and front of the neck. Huge, gaping holes marked the two major injuries, with fourteen satellite stab wounds. The spine in the neck and the spinal cord were three-quarters cut through, an injury that would have required considerable sustained force. The two main arteries in the left side of the neck were completely severed. The adjacent jugular vein was partially severed. The chest showed three further stab wounds.

Edward's family was stunned and extremely distressed by his violent death. He was a loved husband and father who liked a drink but had no history of violence or any other issues in his life that might have been expected to lead him to such a tragic end.

What police found at the scene of this murder made it one of their most easily solved cases, given that such a seemingly random killing could have been so difficult to untangle. The blue wallet under the clubhouse door contained a credit card in the name of 'E Baldock'. A pair of men's shoes lay next to the body, and in the toe of one was a bank key card in the name of 'Miss T Wigginton'. By 10 a.m., police were at an address in a northern suburb of Brisbane, where Tracey answered the door.

How did Tracey Wigginton's key card find its way into the toe of Edward Baldock's shoe? In her first interview with police, the day after the murder, she said she'd lost it the night before when she was frolicking in Orleigh Park with her friends. Later, she recalled picking her card up when she and Edward moved their belongings but could not remember where she'd put it. She had no recollection of putting it into a shoe. Another suggestion produced at trial was that Edward might have picked it up in the dark and thought it was his, so he placed it in his shoe for safekeeping. The most intriguing proposition raised in Tracey's defence was that the card had been deliberately placed in the shoe by one of the multiple personalities inhabiting Tracey's mind—one that hated her violence and wanted to ensure she was caught.

The sequence of events on that October night was pieced together by police largely from accounts given by Tracey's friends rather than by Tracey, as at first she claimed to recall little of what had happened. After leaving the riverside park, Tracey drove to her friends' house and went to sleep. She awoke early and realised she had lost her key card. She and one friend went back to the park to find it, but they saw a man's body, became alarmed, and left. Tracey went home to her own flat and shouted to her girlfriend Debbie, 'I want you in the bedroom right now, I've just seen a dead body!' Debbie drove her to Orleigh Park. By then, police were at the scene, attending to the body. Tracey became distressed and said, 'Oh my God, it's real!' before curling up in the foetal position in the car. The women returned to their flat and Tracey went to sleep after Debbie gave her two sleeping tablets. Three hours later, the police knocked on their door. Debbie was surprised to see how calmly Tracey spoke to them, as if it was all about some minor matter.

Tracey was interviewed three times by police before a charge of murder was laid. In the first interview, she denied knowledge of any murder but admitted having been at Orleigh Park the night before. The police took her there and she showed them the playground area where she said she'd been playing with two friends, and where she must have lost her key card. Police told her it was in that area that a man had just been murdered. She responded, 'Oh, no!' She then told police there had been a third girl present that night—Linda. Tracey hadn't mentioned her before because she didn't want Debbie to know she was seeing Linda.

A second interview was then conducted. Police told Tracey that her friends had told them she'd seen a body the previous night. Tracey became upset and confirmed she had seen the body. It was horrible, she said, and she and her friends hadn't known what to do about it. They were 'scared shitless' and decided not to say anything and just forget about it.

Shortly after that, police interviewed Tracey a third time, telling her that her friends had confessed. She became distressed but, once she was convinced the confession was real, she said, 'Put the tape back in, I'll tell you what happened.' She said her previous two accounts were all lies and then gave a detailed account of the events that resulted in the murder.

Tracey told police that she and her three friends had been at Club Lewmors in Brisbane's nightclub district, drinking Riccadonna spumante. They decided to entice a man down to the river as a joke—Tracey was to turn him on and then leave him there. Then she gave police a detailed account of how she had killed Edward Baldock. Her motives were entirely unclear, but the police had their killer and Tracey was charged and detained in custody. Information was now gathered from friends and family to try to understand what led to the killing, with several people speaking of Tracey's apparent interest in sadism and the occult.

Debbie had been with Tracey for almost two years, but for the six months prior to the killing the relationship was very strained and 'open'. The pair had been planning to go away together to get close again, though Tracey had started an affair with Linda two weeks before the murder. Two days before Edward's death, Tracey had been withdrawn and sullen and spent a lot of time sharpening a knife she owned. The night before the murder, she dyed her hair 'midnight black'.

Her more recent friends reported that Tracey had told them she was a vampire. Linda said Tracey told her she would get pig and cow blood from the butcher to drink. Four times Tracey had persuaded Linda to cut her wrists so that she could suck her blood. Before the killing, she talked about her need to 'feed' and indicated she would drink the victim's blood. However, the three friends who were with her that night did not witness her doing so. They were too scared to leave the car when Tracey took Baldock down to the riverbank—she threatened that if anyone touched her during the process, she was liable to rip their arm off. They had been reluctant to believe Tracey would murder but were convinced by the smell of blood on her breath after the event.

In the weeks before the killing, Tracey and her friends had picnicked at night in the old Toowong cemetery, just west of the city, and had taken home a fallen headstone. The friends felt controlled by Tracey. They believed she had some kind of supernatural power. She had told them to sit cross-legged in front of her and hold eye contact, with the light behind her. They saw Tracey's body disappear, leaving just two cat's eyes floating before them. In the week before the murder, Tracey and one friend had watched a vampire movie in which a couple was abducted and killed. They had also watched, over and over again, a video of someone having their head blown off by a shotgun.

Another friend, Katherine, reported that Tracey often drew faces that were half-animal, half-human. Many times she drew a star inside a circle, or a cross with a rounded top; she had jewellery with these designs. Tracey told Katherine she was fascinated by 'the other side'. She seemed unfeeling and cruel to animals. Several times she had wondered out loud what it would feel like to kill somebody. She would replay many times the scenes in horror movies where people were killed or maimed. She would draw patterns in blood from defrosted meat or from cuts she had made to herself. She told Katherine that she had a 'burning hatred' for her birth mother, who would pay—she would get her.

Dianne, her adoptive sister, reported that when Tracey was in Grade 9 or 10, she read books about witchcraft. In her teens, she loved wearing black clothes, and she drew grotesque, tortured, twisted faces. Stepsister Miriam said that, as a child, Tracey would curl up in the foetal position in an apparent trance for hours when very upset, a behaviour others said persisted into her adult life. She had asked Miriam about black magic and persuaded her to take her to a séance. She asked about the devil and human sacrifices. But as far as Miriam knew, there was no interest in vampirism, and she thought Tracey used to feel sick at the sight of blood.

Another friend indicated that Tracey had spoken of her interest in witchcraft, including the contemporary Wicca movement. She had earlier been very involved in Christianity, but that part of her life was replaced by her darker fascinations. Tracey once cut a pentagon into the back of one of her hands but later covered it with a round tattoo.

Some of the accounts given by friends indicated Tracey's tendency to present differently at certain times in her life. After school she went to TAFE, where she cut her hair very short and spiky and dressed in black. She began answering to the name of Bobby, a persona she took with her when she later moved north to Cairns to work as a bartender and bouncer at a club. Bobby was masculine and tough, even speaking in a deeper voice. She was said at times to wear a studded collar and wristbands, high boots, a black jacket with chrome chains, and gloves with studs on the knuckles. She carried a knife in one boot. To complete the tough image, she rode a motorcycle. Understandably, she developed a fearsome reputation among the nightclub's clientele.

However, this persona did not manifest at home, where friends reported that Tracey was her 'normal' self. Indeed, the persona of Bobby came and went for short periods. (Tracey later insisted to me that this was simply a role she assumed to facilitate her work as a bouncer.) Debbie said that, at times, Tracey was positively childlike, that she would carry a tattered, dirty pillowcase that she called her 'security blanket'. She could also be reclusive, barely emerging from her room for days on end.

There was at least one period in her life when Tracey took on a subservient masochistic role, in contrast to the tough man Bobby. This was when she was in a brief relationship with Billie, a female dominatrix. She wore a collar with a lock and chain attached, by which Billie led her around. Tracey told Debbie that she had allowed Billie to beat her with a strap.

Given the nature of the murder of Edward Baldock, the defence solicitor decided to have Tracey assessed to see if she was mentally ill, anticipating a potential psychiatric defence to the charge. In the first few interviews with a psychiatrist, Tracey was adamant that she had no psychiatric problems, but it eventually became clear that Tracey had little recall of many aspects of her early life. She also had little memory of the night of the murder, despite having confessed in some detail to police. Because of these 'significant amnesias', and after six months of interviews, the psychiatrist began to suspect that he might be dealing with multiple personality disorder (MPD).

Amnesia involving large slabs of time or sequences of behaviour, occurring in the absence of a brain disorder or relevant medical condition, is usually the result of a psychological process called dissociation. The mind is capable of repressing traumatic memories and walling them off in the unconscious. In extreme cases, this can result in the splitting of the mind into distinct sections, which can take on the appearance of separate personalities, or 'alters'. The defence psychiatrist suspected this when he encountered such large memory gaps in Tracey's history and possible evidence of different personas. He recommended to Tracey's lawyers that they gather collateral evidence from other sources and engage an expert—an academic psychologist—to explore the periods of amnesia through interviews under hypnosis. By inducing a hypnotic trance, it was hoped that Tracey would gain access to repressed memories or reveal the presence of other personality states. Tracey was initially reluctant to proceed down this path but eventually agreed. Together, the two professionals subsequently carried out some fifty hypnotic interviews, all of which were videotaped.

Tracey was found to be an excellent hypnotic subject. She went into a deep trance, with no sign of simulation or pretence. Under hypnosis, she was able to recall a great deal about the sexual abuse she had experienced as a child, as well as much more of the events and emotions associated with the murder. She also was able to recount a bizarre episode involving animal sacrifice on Mount Archer, which was near Rockhampton on the coast of central Queensland and apparently notorious for strange gatherings.

Convinced that what they were seeing were 'subtle manifestations of alters', the interviewers began asking to speak to the alters during a number of hypnosis sessions. By asking such questions as 'Is there anyone else there who would like to speak to us?', they courted criticism from other expert witnesses in the trial that they might have encouraged the alters to develop in a person who was in a very suggestible state. Nonetheless, over the course of the hypnotic sessions, the assessors believed they had found evidence of six different alters:

1. Big Tracey—possibly a confederation of alters.
2. Bobby—said to be sixteen, and initially aggressive, contemptuous, cynical and callous. Later, it was thought Bobby might have been present after Tracey was sexually abused and then grew chronologically. Bobby described Big Tracey as 'anxious, depressed, distressed by the murder, and a wimp'.
3. The Observer—called herself 'Me' and watched what the other alters were up to.

4. Little Tracey—a frightened child who was there after the sexual abuse but then did not appear anymore.

5. April—a terrifying alter noted after a 'dramatic disintegration' of Bobby. She appeared to be in control of Bobby by causing screaming in her head. The assessors thought that April might have played an important part on the night of the murder.

6. The Host Personality—the person met outside the hypnosis, regarded as a probable amalgam.

I had two long interviews with Tracey at the Brisbane Women's Correctional Centre at Woolloongabba, assessing her at the request of the court. I was asked to make a diagnosis of any psychiatric disorder and give my opinion regarding any potential mental health defences relevant to the murder charge. By the time I saw her she had already undergone many months of hypnotic interviews—I had seen the videos of those sessions and also had access to all the police material.

Knowing all the details of the horrific offence, I was not sure what I would find when I met Tracey. She was a large young woman, by then twenty-five years old, wide about the hips and thighs. Her face was disarmingly pleasant and her gaze direct. She was polite and her language skills were good. She seemed intelligent. She knew exactly what she was charged with.

Tracey was initially suspicious of me, believing I was there for the prosecution and therefore biased against her, but once I explained my independent role, she cooperated. She concentrated well throughout our two sessions and her thoughts flowed normally, though she was a little anxious and smoked cigarettes. At no stage was there any suggestion of her switching into a different personality state, but there was a certain mechanical style to her account. She used identical phrases and sentences when describing the same incident on different occasions. This gave her account a rehearsed quality, as if she had given it many times before and was performing it yet again for me.

Despite the awful content of her history, Tracey showed virtually no emotion; she shed no tears. The only sign of what might have been beneath the calm facade was anger in her voice when describing her mistreatment by others, particularly her recent problems with Debbie. There was never any hint of psychotic symptoms such as delusions or hallucinations, either in the present or the past. I was intrigued, however, when she told me that she could not recall the name of the psychiatrist who had interviewed her at least sixty times, but described the fact that his glasses were always dirty. She knew other names, so what was it that caused her to suppress the psychiatrist's name? Had he become identified in her mind with things he had uncovered that she wished to forget?

Tracey told me she had little recollection of the third police interview. When she watched the tape of the interview, she saw someone who did not seem like her, more like a stranger who had no emotion and spoke in a dead monotone. All she could now recall were 'brief flashes, like one of those flicker books'. She reported being furious with her girlfriend Debbie in the period leading up to the murder. She felt she had given everything to Debbie, spoilt her with expensive gifts and bent to her every whim, only to be repaid by having to listen to Debbie having sex with other lovers in the room next to hers. Later, she was able to admit that she felt murderous. At first she could not vent that rage directly onto Debbie, or any female friends, but it got to the point where she couldn't handle her anger towards her girlfriend any longer. She said, 'If I'd stayed in the house that night, I think it would have been her that got killed.'

Tracey denied all the reports of vampirism or occult interests. She said the other girls were making it up. I told her that Debbie said that after the offence she found a bag belonging to Tracey that contained a feather, candles wrapped in a black silk cloth, a pack of tarot cards wrapped in a similar cloth, and a large bone that looked like the rib of an animal, which was blackened or burnt on the pointed end. Tracey said Debbie was lying.

She told me about her complex family. She was born in Rockhampton, a regional city some 600 kilometres north of Brisbane. The marriage between her parents, Rachel and Tim, did not appear to last long, and when Rachel became very ill with asthma she struggled as her daughter's sole carer. When Tracey was seven years old, Rachel arranged for her to be adopted by her grandparents, April and Greg. Tracey thus legally became the adoptive sister of her mother.

By the time of the murder, Tracey's adoptive parents were both dead. Greg had been a hardworking man with his own large earth-moving business. As a young child, Tracey had idolised him and he indulged her with anything she wanted. However, as she grew into adulthood, she began to feel intense hatred for him. As an adult she could not recall many details of her childhood, or even get a clear picture in her mind of what Greg looked like. She had pushed memories of him down and avoided thinking about them because 'they made me sick to my stomach'. She had a particular mental image of Greg's large hands touching her. By the time I interviewed her, possibly having retrieved more memories under hypnosis, Tracey had decided her adoptive father was 'a cunt, who deserved to be dead'.

Tracey's description of April was hardly more flattering than that of Greg: 'self-centred, hard, cynical, manipulative and a bitch'. Tracey believed that April must have known of Greg's behaviour but turned a blind eye. Others later described Tracey as being indulged by April.

Besides her sister/mother Rachel, Tracey also had an adoptive sister, Dianne, who was not a biological relation. Tracey's attitude to Rachel had been very negative, indeed hateful, when she was a teenager; she had huge resentment that Rachel had not loved her and had given her away. But as Tracey grew older, and certainly by the time I interviewed her, she could see the adoption from a more understanding perspective. Still, underneath that more mature understanding, I sensed a quite intense continuing ambivalence in her feelings towards Rachel.

There was a third girl in the household, a foster sister called Miriam who was never formally adopted. Miriam was 'the whipping boy' of the family, subject to scapegoating and severe beatings, particularly from April, until she ran away at fifteen. Tracey saw the beatings. At one point April discovered that Greg had had an affair. At about the same time she was injured in a car accident. Those events made her stricter, harder, more vicious, particularly towards Miriam. She would beat the girl up to four times a day with a razor strap or ironing cord. Once, April tied Miriam to a post under the house with the dogs and left her there overnight. Miriam was also punished by April for misdeeds she was blamed for by Tracey. Miriam had reported that two friends of the family had sexually assaulted her. Tracey did not know about those assaults, but she told me she was fairly sure that Greg sexually abused Miriam.

Tracey was sent to private schools in Rockhampton. She hated the first school she attended up until Grade 10 and failed her exams that year. Greg died that same year and Tracey truanted a lot for two months. She was moved to a different school and her marks were a lot better in Grade 11, but after April died she lost interest and left. She could not recall any fights at school and was not severely disciplined. At age eighteen and again at twenty-one, Tracey inherited assets from her adoptive parents and subsequently never had to work to support herself. However, she did choose to work occasionally as a bar attendant or bouncer. In the months before the murder she had also been doing a course in sheet-metal work and enjoying it.

Tracey's sexual and relationship history was chaotic. After her adoptive parents died, she went to live with her birth mother, until they argued and Tracey threw a knife. She moved in with friends of Rachel's, Katherine and her husband Ron, with whom she lived until she turned eighteen. During that time Tracey entered into a relationship with Ron and she became pregnant. It was difficult to arrange an abortion in Queensland at that time, so Ron paid for Tracey to travel hundreds of kilometres to Tweed Heads, across the border in New South Wales. She made the journey alone, and when she returned the relationship with Ron continued.

Katherine's daughter then informed Tracey that Ron had abused her. When Tracey passed that information on to Katherine, she evicted Ron from the household. As if to increase Tracey's confusion, Katherine then drew Tracey into a sexual relationship, which was her initiation into lesbianism. But before long, Katherine, evidently undecided about her own sexuality, started a relationship with a man, prompting Tracey to leave the toxic household.

Tracey went north and met her next girlfriend, Summer. They were together on and off for about two tumultuous years, including three months in Canada. At one stage, the pair keen to be parents, Tracey deliberately got pregnant by having sex with the chosen father in front of their friends, but to her distress she miscarried. After Summer had spent $74 000 of Tracey's money, she lost interest in her girlfriend and left to exploit somebody else. Tracey went into hibernation back in Rockhampton for the next eighteen months. It was during a visit to friends in the country that she met Debbie and they lived together in Queensland's mid-north for eighteen months before moving to Brisbane six months before the murder.

Tracey had always had a bad temper. She tried to keep her anger under control, but there were a number of notable incidents where it boiled over. As a child, Tracey had been violent towards Miriam. One day, they were sitting at a piano, Tracey trying to practise but angry that she wasn't doing well. To vent her rage, she picked up a knitting needle and stabbed it through Miriam's thigh, causing permanent scarring.

When Tracey was fifteen she assaulted a family friend called Keith, a verbally abusive alcoholic who was trying to get close to April after Greg died. He was sitting on a couch with April when he ran his hand up April's leg. She rebuffed him, and Keith slapped her. Tracey was furious and in an outwardly calm way viciously attacked Keith. He ended up with blackened eyes, a fractured nose, and his hearing aid driven into his ear canal. She also slashed his fingers with a knife. She completely forgot about the assault until years later, when the memory flashed back as she was moving furniture in the room where the incident had occurred.

At sixteen, a few months after April died, there was another destructive outburst. This time it was triggered when Tracey went to her sister Dianne's house and found almost all of her late adoptive mother's household belongings stored in the garage, along with her car. She recalled having heard her two sisters planning the division of April's things between them while their mother lay dying in hospital. Yet Tracey had been the one who'd provided care to her adoptive mother in her last days—she felt her sisters had done nothing. Now she had nothing left apart from bad memories, and, seeing all her mother's belongings stashed away at Dianne's house, Tracey went berserk. She smashed all the furniture, tipped the fridge over, ruined the paintings. She destroyed everything except the car, which she left untouched because she had good memories of riding in it with April. When she'd finished, she walked calmly from the house as if nothing had happened. Five days later, Rachel confronted Tracey about what she'd done. Tracey had no immediate recall of the rampage—the memory only gradually returned as she was reminded of what had happened.

Summer was also the victim of Tracey's temper. As Tracey put it to me in an interview, 'there were three times I beat the living crap out of her'. These assaults occurred after a build-up of anger, when Tracey felt that Summer was being uncaring, nagging or obstructive. They were carried out coolly and methodically, twice causing nose fractures and other facial injuries.

Two weeks before the murder, Tracey entered into an intense, tempestuous relationship with Linda, who would be charged as a co-offender in Edward Baldock's murder. I learnt that Tracey had seriously assaulted Linda in custody. Tracey thought Linda was taunting her and she became increasingly angry. One day she got Linda alone and put a hand around her neck, pushing her up against a wall. Linda was blue in the face by the time prison officers intervened. Once again, Tracey had no recall of the episode until she saw Linda again and was told what she'd done.

When Tracey discussed her violence with me, she said that her anger took a long while to build up, but that when it boiled over she completely lost control. She was frightened by how she could be so aggressive and yet express it with such apparent nonchalance and outward calmness. Intellectually, she saw herself as opposed to violence, and therefore she felt afraid of the potential for extreme aggression that she had so amply demonstrated. But as she told me about her violent episodes, about what she had done to people, I detected a hint of relish. I thought this indicated a degree of sadism, getting pleasure from inflicting pain. What she said about not liking violence did not always correlate with how she came across as she described her actions in vivid detail.

Tracey also told me about the significant event she'd witnessed on Mount Archer. She'd forgotten about it until it was raised by the defence psychiatrist, who had in turn learned about it through a friend who had taken Tracey to a party on the mountain when she was about eighteen.

Tracey and her friend had driven into a clearing—she recalled a fire and a group of people dressed in cassocks. A man arrived in a truck that had a white goat in the back. While the other people stood around him in a semi-circle—except for Tracey, who stayed in the car—the man pulled back the goat's head and Tracey's friend cut its neck with a knife. A cup was passed around the group and Tracey presumed it contained the goat's blood. Tracey then told her friend she wanted to leave and they drove to a tavern.

Tracey told me the whole episode intrigued her but also sickened her—she remembered having to stop on the way home to vomit by the roadside. She claimed to hate cruelty to animals. I told her that other reports I had read about her were divided about that. Some said she was kind, while others described her as cruel and callous; some even suggested she might have been responsible for the death of a Persian cat she'd once owned. Tracey could only recall the cat disappearing one day.

Tracey's case was referred by her lawyers to Queensland's Mental Health Court, a special part of the state's Supreme Court that was set up to hear cases where a psychiatric defence might be relevant, or where fitness for trial was at issue. The defence put forward their case, based on the reports of their psychiatrist and psychologist, that Tracey was suffering from MPD, a condition they thought sufficient to qualify as a mental disorder under the law and had deprived her of control of her actions at the time of the offence. Such an opinion, if upheld by the court, would mean a finding of unsoundness of mind (elsewhere known as not guilty by reason of insanity).

In response to this referral, three further psychiatric reports were solicited by the parties involved and the court itself. Thus, by the time of the hearing, there would be four psychiatrists and one psychologist giving evidence. Many lawyers might cynically say that this would likely give rise to five different opinions. In fact, this was rather like the actual outcome, although there was quite a lot of overlap between the opinions.

Tracey did not deny the fact that she had killed Edward Baldock, but the matter up for decision was whether, at that time, she was deprived of any of three relevant capacities: to know what she was doing, to know it was wrong, or to control her actions. If Tracey was found not to have been deprived, the next step would be to determine if she had substantial impairment of the capacities, which would produce a defence of diminished responsibility, reducing the charge to one of manslaughter. Finally, if she were not unsound, the court would determine fitness for trial. If fit, she would go back to trial in the mainstream Supreme Court, most likely for a simple sentencing hearing. If she did get a defence of unsoundness, she would be placed on a forensic order and become an involuntary patient in a secure hospital under the forensic provisions of the *Mental Health Act*. Criminal proceedings would then be discontinued.

Tracey's case was complicated. Explaining why she murdered Edward Baldock, a stranger to her, in the way that she did, was not easy. The experts tried to draw together all the strands of Tracey's life and experiences to provide some coherent explanation. There was common ground in the opinions that Tracey had experienced a lot of childhood trauma that had left her severely scarred emotionally. She had evidence of a significant personality disorder, problems with anger, and a history of significant violence, albeit with no formal past criminal history. There was less agreement when it came to MPD.

MPD is a controversial diagnosis. It became prevalent in the mid-twentieth century when psychoanalysis held sway as a popular form of therapy, particularly in America. It was a source of great fascination and formed the plot for Hollywood movies and TV shows such as *The Three Faces of Eve* and *Sybil*. So common did it become that professionals came to realise the condition could actually be induced by intensive psychotherapy, encouraged by suggestions from the therapist seeking possible alters in traumatised patients. This was even more likely if hypnosis was used, because that increased the suggestibility of the patient even more. Some psychiatrists are of the view that MPD is iatrogenic—always caused by the therapy. Certainly, as psychoanalysis fell out of favour, the frequency of MPD also diminished and that diagnosis is now rarely made, except by a few die-hard believers. Most psychiatrists will indicate that they have only ever seen one or two genuine cases of MPD where therapy has not been involved as a potential cause. Some claim never to have seen it. Nowadays, traumatised individuals will more likely be diagnosed with post-traumatic stress disorder or borderline personality disorder. MPD has even lost its original name. It is now classified as dissociative identity disorder (DID) in an effort to better describe the role of dissociation in the production of alters.

Tracey's case occurred towards the end of the period of MPD's popularity as a diagnosis—the defence psychiatrist had practised during the latter part of its heyday. At the trial, the defence team and one other psychiatrist gave the opinion that MPD had been present prior to the murder and had a significant effect on Tracey's capacities. I gave the opinion that it was possible Tracey did have MPD, but that it had been shaped and produced in its final form only as a result of the assessment process, through the use of hypnosis and suggestion. I noted that Tracey seemed to often use the mechanism of dissociation to block out memories of traumatic events from her conscious mind. A fourth psychiatrist did not accept that Tracey had MPD, which in any case he believed only ever existed when caused by therapy. He diagnosed a personality disorder.

In a comprehensive 33-page judgment, the judge summarised the evidence received by the court. He indicated that much had been heard on two issues—first, the status of multiple personality, and second, the use of hypnosis. In regard to multiple personality, he detailed the differences of opinion given in evidence, which reflected similar controversy in world opinion. He noted that the primary classification system of mental diseases then in use (the third edition of the *Diagnostic and Statistical Manual of Mental Disorders*) had a foreword cautioning that the presence of a disorder in a psychiatric classification did not mean that it was necessarily relevant to the legal considerations involving the relationship between illness and legal competencies.

He neatly resolved this issue as follows:

> The Court regards the status of multiple personality disorder as controversial. It is not its function to resolve controversies among psychiatrists, but to make a determination as to the mental condition of the patient at the time when the alleged offence was committed. For this purpose it does not find it necessary either to accept or reject the concept of multiple personality disorder as

a specific entity. Its concern is to determine, on the basis of the evidence put before it, whether the patient was suffering at the time from unsoundness of mind or diminished responsibility, and whether the patient is fit for trial.

The judge also discussed the use of hypnosis at some length. He noted that an account of the killing taken under hypnosis couldn't necessarily be taken to reflect the actual mental state of the offender during the killing. What is said under hypnosis cannot be seen as 'truer' than an account outside of hypnosis. An account of an event under hypnosis might be a reliving, but it could be some-one else's account. It might be a response to suggestion or a rep-etition of a fantasy. There was also the big issue of the interviewer shaping the account given and even assisting in the manufacture of a multiple personality.

The judge concluded:

> Even if at the time of the alleged offence the patient was in a state of mental disease or natural mental infirmity, it did not deprive her of capacity to understand what she was doing, or of capacity to control her actions, or of capacity to know that she ought not do the act.

Similarly, the court was not persuaded that Tracey satisfied the criteria for a defence of diminished responsibility:

> It accepts that, even if she had multiple personality disorder, in addition to a significant personality disorder, it did not substantially impair her capacities … the evidence leads to a conclusion on the balance of probabilities that she knew at the time what she was doing, that she had planned it with a degree of care, and that she knew it was wrong to do the act. Her background of early sexual abuse and family violence may have contributed to make her a violent person, and she was clearly angry on the night of the

killing, but the evidence does not satisfy the Court that she was at the time of the killing in a state of abnormality of mind (as used in the Criminal Code).

The judge declared Tracey fit for trial and remanded her in custody to await an appearance in the mainstream Supreme Court. Tracey subsequently pleaded guilty to murder and was sentenced to life imprisonment, to serve a minimum of thirteen years before parole. She was finally released after her fourth bid for parole, in January 2012, twenty-one years after her imprisonment.

Media reports gave this case huge publicity, with Tracey nicknamed 'The Lesbian Vampire Killer'. It was reported that while in prison Tracey completed a Bachelor of Arts from Deakin University in Victoria, majoring in philosophy and anthropology. She completed trade certificates to drive bobcats and forklifts and to do welding. She was also reported to have used heroin in custody for five years, contracting hepatitis C from a dirty needle. In 2006 she reportedly assaulted a fellow inmate while at a prison farm and was returned to a high-security prison for a period of time.

Photos published in the press on the day of her release showed her to be frail and walking with the aid of crutches. To me, she looked much like she did years earlier—just older, by then forty-five; greyer; and not quite so mobile.

The Courier Mail newspaper published an account of an interview with Tracey in 1996, when she was still in prison. About her crime, Tracey is reported to have said:

I had snapped. I knew I couldn't kill a woman or someone I knew, but I don't know what I was looking for ... I can still smell the river—it was really salty smelling—the smell of blood, the smell of metal that had been left to rust in the rain. And it was a cold night, very cold ... You think nothing. Nothing goes through your mind. There is no emotion, just blind fury. Murder is a terrifying experience—it's extremely scary to have that much power. It's playing God, with life and death. Nobody should have that sort of power ... but we all do.

Tracey's case was important as a legal precedent because it made clear statements about the status of dissociation and multiple personality when it comes to legal responsibility. It made clear that the whole person, not any one alter, bears responsibility for a crime. It helped to clarify the difference between extreme expressions of emotion such as anger, and behaviour arising from a significant mental illness. It also cast serious doubt upon the validity of using hypnosis as a tool to gather evidence for use in legal matters.

Tracey's case illustrated the power of emotions arising from past traumas in shaping future relationships and behaviour. Buried rage does not always stay buried, despite all the strategies the mind might employ to keep it down. In killing poor Edward Baldock, Tracey took revenge on all her past abusers. He was an innocent man but became for Tracey the lightning rod that focused all of her bile and rage. He became Greg and Rachel and Ron and Katherine and Summer and Debbie. When Tracey told me that her adoptive father deserved to be dead, I felt she seemed at the same time to be talking about Edward Baldock, as the personification of Greg and all the others.

There was a disturbing callousness to Tracey's violence, perhaps borrowed from the same callousness she had observed when her adoptive mother repeatedly thrashed Miriam. In order for someone to be that violent, there has to be at some level an acceptance of such behaviour as justified; that is, unless serious mental illness destroys one's normal empathies. Tracey had no such illness. Her innate killer instinct was released by overwhelming rage welling up from her past and influencing her present—visiting that rage upon an unfortunate victim who in her mind became the embodiment of all her past traumas.

Tracey was, and is, a complex person. Having not seen her for twenty-seven years, I cannot say to what extent she has dealt with the issues that gave rise to Edward Baldock's murder. Statistics would suggest that, by now, the risk of further serious violence, especially murder, is much reduced by her age and the effects of a long period in custody. An enraged murder such as Baldock's is generally a one-off event, unlikely to occur again. Queensland's Parole Board has made that assessment. Tracey is now in the community and will be under parole supervision for the rest of her life.

THE MATTER OF MIND AND BRAIN

The question of how the mind relates to the brain is a fascinating one. Is the mind separate from the brain, or are the two simply one? I leave that to others to argue about. All I know is that the mind depends on the brain to exist, and that damage to the brain also damages the mind.

How can we define consciousness? If we have it, we know what it means—an ability to take in our surroundings, to be aware, to interact, reason and make decisions. We also know what it means to lose consciousness—we lose all awareness. That might come about from a blow to the head concussing the brain; from disease in the brain; from disease elsewhere in the body depriving the brain of its needs; or from an anaesthetic or drug intoxication.

In-between full consciousness and unconsciousness there may be degrees of clouding or impairment, during which we will be confused, vague, disoriented and not responding appropriately to our surroundings. This is called delirium, which can have many causes. In such a state, we may behave bizarrely or illegally.

Then there is the concept of the subconscious—that hinterland inside our mind containing thoughts, feelings and memories of which we are not usually aware. In everyday life we have to focus on the task at hand and put other things out of our mind. Those things are just put aside temporarily but readily attended to when we change focus. Other thoughts and emotions may be more deeply suppressed if they involve difficult or complicated matters that we would prefer not to think about, but we can still call to mind with a bit of effort. For all of us, however, there are many things that are more firmly pushed into our unconscious minds, especially painful memories, traumatic events or unacceptable impulses. Those things may come to the fore in dreams, slips of the tongue, or in response to sudden reminders of past events or traumas. Even while buried, these subconscious memories and emotions may influence our ideas and behaviour in ways beyond our ken. From that may come anxiety, phobias, suspicions and prejudices.

Somehow, the mind has this ability to tuck away memories and feelings into the subconscious. We call that by such names as suppression and repression but we have no real idea of the mechanisms involved in that process at the level of the brain. It is a very handy, indeed essential, ability to deal with trauma or unacceptable impulses within ourselves. But a problem might arise when long-buried memories and emotions are suddenly released into our conscious mind. This is particularly so if the emotions released are very strong and angry. The relevance of such a sudden release of rage is evident in two of the cases I describe in this book: that of Tracey Wigginton in Chapter 1, and Leslie Brown in Chapter 9.

The phenomenon of dissociation is an interesting variant of the mind's ability to repress memories or feelings. In its milder forms it may involve a separation of the full awareness of feeling from a traumatic experience, such that what is happening seems dream-like, detached or in slow motion. You might even feel you can see yourself in a traumatic experience as if you are an onlooker. The mind shuts off the feelings associated with the trauma as a protective mechanism.

Dissociation can take another, more severe form, whereby the mind separates a whole segment of traumatic life experience and shuts it off as if in its own box, where it remains hidden in the subconscious. Multiple such separations can give the appearance of multiple personalities, as in the case of Tracey. No matter how deeply buried a trauma may be, it can have an effect on the person's behaviour and relationships in ways of which they are not consciously aware. Sudden violence associated with subsequent amnesia is one possibility. At least one-third of murderers claim amnesia for their offence. Some of them are lying, some were too intoxicated to remember, but some do not remember because their mind has suppressed the traumatic event from their conscious awareness.

2

SADISTIC SECRETS

Grant Meredith had a vague memory of sitting in his car in the early hours of a Sunday morning in 2008. It was still dark. He was looking out over Gladstone, a small industrial port city on the central Queensland coast. Streetlights defined familiar landmarks below his vantage point, a popular parking area atop a small hill that provided a view out to the ocean. He had a strange hollow feeling in his chest. Looking back later, Grant was unable to say whether this was before or after what he did that morning. Most probably, it was from that position he first saw Kathryn Daley as a distant figure leaving a nightclub and walking south out of the centre of town. He would have seen that she was alone. He did not know Kathryn but it seems at that moment he chose her as his target.

Early the following morning, three railway workers began walking beside some train tracks towards a fault up the line that they had been sent to fix. The bush was quite thick either side of the line, but the trio followed a rough track made by vehicles in the past, probably used by pig hunters. They had only gone a few hundred metres before they saw her. She wasn't far off the track, face down, fully clothed, her hands tied with rope behind her back, a huge spreading stain where the blood had soaked into the sandy soil around her head and neck. Without touching her, they could see her neck had been cut from side to side. Flies and ants were crawling over her. She was clearly dead and had been so for some time. The workers called their base and the authorities were quickly on the scene.

Kathryn Daley, who had been reported missing by her parents the day before, was a 21-year-old apprentice electrician, a well-liked local girl who lived with a flatmate not far from her parents' home. That Saturday night she had gone out with a group of her close friends. They started at a pub and later in the night moved on to a nightclub. Kathryn drank, laughed and danced until 4 a.m., when she decided to walk home. Friends offered to drive her, but her flat wasn't far and she wanted to get some fresh air. On the way she phoned to arrange to meet two friends at a service station about a kilometre down the road, to get a burger. That was the last time anyone heard from her—she never arrived. CCTV footage showed Kathryn leaving the nightclub and walking off down the road, but there the coverage ran out. On Sunday, Kathryn wasn't responding to texts or calls to her phone. At 6 p.m. her parents went to the police and lodged a missing person report.

At the gruesome crime scene, and during later examination, police and forensic experts made a number of curious discoveries. Kathryn had her hands tightly bound behind her back. She appeared to have been forced to the ground, her head held back by her hair and her throat deeply cut, causing her death. When found, she was dressed in the shirt and jeans she had been wearing that night, but her underwear, both briefs and bra, was missing. A number of items that she would have had on her that night were also missing: her driver's licence, a bank card, her phone and black Billabong thongs. Even more curious, a torn piece of mauve bra strap was found next to her body, which did not match any bra owned by Kathryn.

Post-mortem examination revealed that Kathryn had been brutally raped. She had suffered a number of injuries to her vaginal and anal areas, with severe bruising and evidence of bleeding. This indicated that those injuries had been inflicted prior to her death. This could only have meant that at some point after Kathryn was abducted she was taken to some secluded place, restrained, undressed and subjected to terrible, painful sexual assaults, before being dressed again, without underwear, and taken to where she was killed. Police surmised that her killer had removed the missing items from the scene and probably disposed of them.

The initial evidence was shocking, especially for Kathryn's family and friends, but it gave no early hint as to the identity of the killer. Kathryn had no known enemies, no estranged or angry ex-partner, and she was not depressed—she loved her job. The murder seemed to be the result of a random abduction by an unknown stranger. He could now be long gone and might never be tracked down.

Of course, no investigation is complete without trying to find DNA evidence. Traces of the DNA of an unknown male were found on the rope and Kathryn's clothing. It did not match any known offender in Queensland, but there was excitement among investigators when a match came from New South Wales. DNA had been gathered some ten years earlier from a break-and-enter offence in suburban Sydney, and the man to which it belonged, Grant Meredith, then twenty years old, had been a person of interest. Police had never managed to charge him for that offence because the victims lived behind the house where he grew up and he had been in their home a number of times. He had a history of drink-driving offences.

Investigations moved into full swing to try to track down Grant Meredith. His parents indicated that their son had gone away about three years earlier to work in the mining industry and they had not heard from him for some time. When he'd last contacted them, he was in the outback Queensland town of Mount Isa but he'd indicated that he was moving on. Inquiries shifted to Mount Isa and his former employer there. Grant had been with them for about two years, but they had had to dismiss him almost a year earlier because he was using alcohol heavily and had become unreliable. Ex-workmates said they thought he'd moved to Gladstone.

Real estate agents there were able to help in locating Grant Meredith. He'd been living in a caravan park until a few days after Kathryn's murder and had then taken up a lease on a small townhouse, where he was still living and paying rent several weeks later. Police established that he worked for the largest mining company in the city as a machine operator. If this was their man, however, why was he still in town? Why had he not hidden himself in some distant place? Covert surveillance mapped Grant's movements and it was determined that an early morning raid would be conducted on his home, with a warrant to search his townhouse and car.

The raid took place at 5 a.m., shortly before Grant was to leave for an early-morning shift, taking him completely by surprise. He was taken in for questioning while the search of his home and belongings began. At the start of the police questioning, he volunteered, 'I think I did it.'

In his bedroom, police found a bag containing a bloodied knife, Kathryn Daley's licence, her phone, her underwear and one of her rubber thongs. A second bag containing Kathryn's bank card was found under the bed. It also held numerous items of female clothing not belonging to Kathryn, and a number of sexual aids. There were at least three dildos, one of them very large. One of the clothing items was a mauve bra with a broken strap, which matched the item found next to Kathryn's body. DNA testing of Kathryn's clothing showed a match with both Kathryn Daley and Grant Meredith.

Among the objects in the second bag was a small piece of yellow paper that looked like a Post-it note. On it was drawn in pencil a grid diagram, possibly a primitive road map. Alongside the most distant line was drawn a small stick figure of a person. When shown that piece of evidence later, Grant denied all knowledge of it or what it might represent. Police thought it was a map indicating where he had left the body, but he denied any plan to use it to return to the scene of the murder.

Grant also had an old computer. A search of the hard drive found thousands of images and several videos of child pornography. The estimated ages of the children involved ranged from fifteen years down to as young as six months of age.

He was charged with one count of murder, one count of rape and two counts of possession of child exploitation material.

I was asked to see Grant Meredith more than two years after he had been charged and incarcerated. By then he had turned thirty-three. The legal system moves slowly in such matters and he was still on remand, awaiting trial. The request came from his legal advisers, who had referred his matter for consideration quite late, after a barrister had reviewed the evidence. The barrister was very troubled by the disturbing nature of the evidence and the fact that Grant could not recall much of what had happened. Grant could not explain why he had kept Kathryn's belongings. He had also revealed a great deal of sexual deviancy. The lawyers wanted to try to get some clarity about any mental health issues, his fitness for trial, and his potential dangerousness.

I looked forward to the challenge of assessing Grant, as I, too, was intrigued by the implications of the material that had been sent to me by his lawyers. I hoped that I might be able to uncover his motivations and achieve greater insights as to what this murder had been about. If I could clarify those things, I would have a much better chance of making an informed risk assessment and determining if mental health issues were relevant to the charges.

I interviewed Grant over a few hours in the Capricornia Correctional Centre, 15 kilometres north of Rockhampton. He was a short man of thickset, muscular build, with short brown hair and light stubble on his face. He was dressed in a prison tracksuit and seemed clean and reasonably well groomed. While polite and superficially cooperative, he was quite guarded and unforthcoming when it came to giving information and explanations. For much of the interview he needed a lot of direct questioning, with little free-flowing account of himself. He indicated that his mood was stable; he had been assessed by the prison mental health service as having no active mental health issues apart from a history of heavy alcohol abuse. During the interview he actually showed very little emotional response to any of the facts of his crime, except to look a little strained when I pressed him to talk about why he committed the offence. He seemed virtually unable to describe his emotions, claiming no particular feelings about even the most sensitive matters. When asked for his feelings about Kathryn and what he had done to her, the most he could offer was 'I wish it hadn't happened', leaving open the question of whether he wished that for his own sake, or for that of his victim.

Grant seemed to me to be of just below average intelligence. There was no indication that he suffered from any kind of brain disease that might affect his memory, nor any symptoms of major psychiatric disorder such as psychosis. He did say, however, that he had very little recall of most of his childhood, and that there were also whole swathes of his adult life he found difficult to remember. Some of this amnesia could have been attributable to very heavy alcohol and drug abuse over many years. But the pattern of his amnesia, whereby he recalled some things clearly but forgot large patches of time, was not really consistent with any organic or illness cause. He had also been able to be employed and look after himself in the community, which would be very difficult if he had real neurologically based memory deficits. If his amnesia was real, it was more suggestive of psychological processes pushing memories of difficult, unacceptable things out of his consciousness.

After getting what I could of Grant's life history spontaneously from him, I turned to a more direct, interrogatory style of interviewing. There were things I needed to know about that he had entirely skipped over or neglected to mention altogether.

His memory of the night of the offence was patchy—he described it as like 'black and white patches of memory'. He had gone to two separate homes that night, to drink, hang out with mates from work, and play pool. He said he would have drunk a bottle of rum and some beer, his usual level of intake when he was not working early the next day. For most people, such an amount of alcohol would lead to very severe intoxication, so for Grant to continue to function, to drive and then carry out an abduction, rape and murder, he clearly must have built up a great tolerance to alcohol and could be diagnosed as alcoholic. Grant eventually gave me a history of very heavy alcohol and drug abuse beginning at age thirteen, including cannabis, speed, LSD, heroin and ice. As a result, his life was 'a blur' for some years. Over the past few years he'd drunk nearly a bottle of spirits a day, timing his intake so as not to disrupt his work—he got the shakes when not drinking but cured those by drinking again.

Grant did recall sitting in his car on top of the hill above Gladstone, and had flashes of seeing a girl in the car, someone with blondish hair and a white shirt, although he couldn't remember telling police she had looked scared. He also recalled driving and being near a crossroad with two signs, then being parked by the side of a road. Grant's next memory was of waking up at home in the morning, feeling sick, somehow knowing something was wrong but unable to work it out. He said, 'It was like a déjà vu feeling, as if something was off.' He was very vague about what he did that day, believing he stayed home. The next day he returned to work and went on with normal life until the police came to arrest him a few weeks later.

But there were other reminders of what he had done. A day or so after the murder, he'd cleaned his car. He found one of his bags under the seat and was shocked and confused to find Kathryn Daley's licence, a phone, female underwear and a bloodied knife inside. At first he didn't know what to make of this discovery, but then he recognised Kathryn's name from the extensive media coverage of her murder. For a long time he didn't want to contemplate that he was Kathryn's killer. He moved from the caravan park, hiding the material in his new townhouse and trying to forget it. When he did think about taking the things to the police, he decided, 'It wouldn't be a good look, they'd think I did it.' However, by the time of his arrest he'd realised he must have done it, hence his early tentative confession.

In those initial interviews with police, Grant agreed that he had Kathryn's items in his possession. He also agreed he had child pornography on his computer, as well as printed images. He told police and his lawyers that he had for years had transvestic sadomasochistic fetishism, whereby he would dress in female clothing and use dildos on himself to experience fantasies of sexual humiliation. However, he denied having any fantasies involving sexual violence. He claimed to be a non-violent person. He had never had any connection with Kathryn Daley prior to abducting her.

I tried to explore these things further with Grant, but he was very vague. He even got his victim's surname slightly wrong, calling her 'Delany'. He said he had been fine in the period leading up to the murder—going to work as normal, socialising with his friends. He was even hazy about the exact charges he was facing and the evidence that had been gathered against him, despite having repeatedly spoken to his lawyers. There was still an evident effort on his part to avoid thinking about anything to do with his offence.

Grant's parents, both recently retired, lived in an outer suburb of Sydney. He had never got on with his metalworker father and avoided him. He also clashed with his mother, a nurse. There was a lot of shouting but no physical violence. Both parents were moderate drinkers. He had one sister, married with kids, and they had been quite close. No-one in Grant's family had a criminal history. He guessed his parents were shocked by his offence but he had not talked to them about it, even when they had made a visit to see him in prison.

It was hard to discern why Grant could remember so little of his childhood, particularly as he denied experiencing any abuse, either physical or sexual. What did become clear was that he was in trouble all the time at school, with his parents often called in for a chat, and he had to repeat Grade 3. He progressed to a boys-only Catholic high school but was expelled in Grade 9 after a big fight involving a number of boys—the fact that he was the only one kicked out suggested that he was seen as the ringleader. His second Catholic high school lasted one term of frequent truanting before he was told not to return. He ended up in a state high school in Grade 10 but he was rebellious, got into fights, and was again expelled.

His father wangled him an apprenticeship in sheet-metal work, but lack of motivation, drug use and unreliability meant that lasted less than a year. For much of the next ten years Grant lived a life of intoxicated instability on the dole, supplemented by a little drug trafficking and probably stealing, but his only official offences involved drink driving. Eventually, three years before Kathryn's murder, he managed to start supporting himself with legitimate work in the mining industry, albeit with ongoing alcohol abuse that caused problems at times. He made some friends who also worked and lived normal lives.

Superficially, Grant's sex life was fairly unremarkable. He had had about five or six relationships with women around his own age since high school, lasting for up to a year. He had never reached the stage of cohabiting and had no children. The last relationship of any significance was before he took on the mining job. Sex with these women was 'normal', with no unusual or kinky practices.

His secret sex life was quite different. He couldn't say how or why it began, but at some stage in his teens, Grant started dressing in female clothing, which he collected from clothing bins and would hide in his room. More and more, when alone and assured of privacy in his parent's home, he would cross-dress and become sexually aroused by doing so. On a few occasions he ventured from the house wearing female underwear, but he never went out in full female garb. Having no mirror in his room, he would take photographs of himself dressed as a woman and look at them later.

While dressed as a woman, Grant revelled in vivid fantasies of himself being humiliated. He would imagine a woman, occasionally a man, laughing at him, pointing at him, ordering him to do things to himself. He went to sex shops and obtained dildos of various sizes. He would insert the dildos into his anus and imagine his humiliators sodomising him. He did not experience this as violent or painful. It was just pleasurable—he would masturbate to ejaculation.

This sexual activity happened about twice a week over many years. Afterwards, he would wonder where it all came from, but he just took it as an acceptable practice that did no harm to anyone. He never told anyone else about it. Over the years, he had visited prostitutes about fifteen times and would have liked them to act out a humiliation scenario, but he never had the courage to ask. He had fantasised about a threesome with a woman and a man but had no interest in homosexual sex.

Using the internet, he had nurtured an interest in child pornography and collected quite a lot. He liked viewing children having sex with adults but said he never wanted to masturbate to those images. It was more a matter of curiosity. He did enjoy, and masturbate to, images or videos of men being humiliated by a dominatrix mistress.

I tried to draw Grant out to gain some understanding of the motives for Kathryn's murder. He denied violent fantasies or mental rehearsals of the crime. He seemed quite concerned about his lack of understanding, as no clues had come to mind over the time since the offence. He had not experienced any dreams or nightmares about what had happened, and had no clue about the small map with the stick figure on it; he didn't even recall the police questioning him about it. He also denied using Kathryn's clothing for sexual stimulation or cross-dressing—he could not explain why he had kept it.

Finally, I asked Grant if he had ever done anything like the offence before. I was very disturbed by the similarities between his behaviour and that of serial sadistic rapists or murderers. His answer didn't really provide me with much reassurance. He at first said, 'No.' When I asked if he was certain about that, he replied, 'I have to be certain, because there are so many parts of my life I don't remember. I hope not, it's not me.' I was left wondering how many Kathryns there might have been, murders never solved. I hoped there were none and that the modern miracle of DNA had managed to stop Grant before he could repeat his actions.

Clearly, the evidence was overwhelming when presented at the committal hearing. When the trial moved on to the Supreme Court, Grant Meredith pleaded guilty to all charges. He was sentenced to two years' imprisonment for the child pornography offences, twelve years for the rape and a mandatory life sentence for the murder. The result is that he is now in a place where at least the community is protected.

Since Grant was so guarded and apparently lacking in any insights into his emotions and behaviour, I was left to speculate about what he did, and why. These speculations would not have been of much use to his lawyer in the legal processes. While Grant was clearly sexually perverse and an alcoholic, he did not have any other diagnosable mental illness that might offer any kind of defence for his actions. He understood enough, and was intelligent enough, to instruct his lawyer and to make a plea. He was able to attend and follow court proceedings. Therefore, he was fit for trial. He had given very few clues as to influences that might have shaped his perverted and violent behaviour, so no coherent explanation for his offending would be available to the court. In any case, a conviction for murder would result in a mandatory life sentence, so no mitigating factors would be taken into account. My speculations were therefore for my own academic interest and the clinical challenge Grant represented.

In regard to what he did, it was clear he chose his victim at random, with no thought for her humanity—at best, with no empathy at all for how she might suffer; at worst, making her suffer was a necessary part of his motivation. It appeared that Grant first restrained Kathryn at a site separate from where the killing occurred, and sexually assaulted her very violently. The injuries were so severe that they could not have been caused by a penis. A larger, more damaging object was used, and the image of the huge dildo in his bag inevitably comes to mind. He then dressed Kathryn, or made her dress herself, minus her underwear, which he put into his bag, before killing her near the railway tracks.

There are many unanswered questions. At the murder scene, a piece of a bra strap—presumably his—was found. Why would that be there? Did he put it on? Did he take any other items of his female clothing there to wear? Was he dressed as a woman during these ghastly actions? Was the killing of Kathryn part of the whole process, part of the thrill, or was it just to silence her? Did he take Kathryn's things as souvenirs, as trophies? Were the other items of female clothing he had in his possession really taken from clothing bins, or could the awful alternative explanation be that those items were souvenirs from earlier victims?

We know about Grant's transvestism and his masochistic wish to be humiliated, acted out by him in his bedroom using the props he had accumulated, but we don't know the origins of this. He said he accepted it all, and showed little concern or feeling about it, but it had been a tightly held secret. What if, at a deeper level, he was much more conflicted about these perverse sexual drives than he was willing to admit consciously?

Masochism is one side of a coin, on the other side of which is sadism. The masochist gets pleasure from being hurt; the sadist gets pleasure from hurting. It is not impossible that these apparently opposite sides show up in the same person. During his lone sexual acts, Grant dressed as a female and gained pleasure from being humiliated. But he was also acting out the role of the sadist, usually also a female, gaining pleasure from inflicting the humiliation. Was it possible for Grant to have become so conflicted and angry about his need to become a humiliated female that he needed to kill off that part of himself? Could he have humiliated Kathryn in ways he had humiliated himself in fantasy so often in the past, then killed her as a symbolic way of killing off the submissive woman inside him, whom he had come to despise? Did the sadistic drive become so strong that his fantasy was no longer enough to satisfy him, so that he had to seek out a real female to enact the fantasy and make it reality? This progression from powerful fantasy and imagined rehearsal to actual sadistic sexual assault or murder is the usual path for the sadistic killer.

The fact that Grant was found in possession of child pornography would suggest that paedophilia was another possible diagnosis. He tended to downplay any great interest in sex with children himself, but he gained some kind of pleasure from seeing adults having sex with children. My impression was that his interest might have been an extension of his sadistic drive, seeing children being subverted and dominated, rather than true paedophilia. Another possibility would be that he had actually been sexually abused as a child but repressed that memory. Viewing child pornography might have been a kind of acting out of his own experiences. In any case, from his account, the interest in child pornography had largely been supplanted in recent years by his transvestic and sadomasochistic preoccupations. Multiple sexual paraphilias are commonly seen together in the one person, evolving from one to another over time. The peeping tom may move on to flashing, then progress to being a rapist.

Since Grant is unable, or unwilling, to give us any insights, these questions about his case will probably never be answered. He will spend many years in prison. He may be assessed as to his suitability for one of the sexual offender treatment programs offered in prison, but having been sentenced to life he would be seen as a low priority until closer to his release date many years hence. Prisons have limited resources and few professionals able to explore all these scenarios. Precious treatment dollars will likely be spent on sex offenders who are more likely to respond to rehabilitative measures, rather than on someone doing life for a sadistic murder.

Understanding the origins of sexual sadism and sexual murder is difficult. Sometimes there are obvious childhood influences and experiences, which might include extreme cruelty and sexual abuse by carers. Mostly, however, the reasons for the drives and behaviours remain much more obscure than the descriptions of the behaviours themselves. For someone to progress to rape and killing, sexual drive alone is generally not enough. That perverse sexual drive, whatever its origin, has to be accompanied by quite profound emotional and personality disorder, usually of the psychopathic kind. The psychopath is incapable of empathy for others, self-centred and exploitative, and feels no guilt or shame. Combine those features with perverse sexual interests and you have a potentially deadly mix. Grant's inability to feel or express emotion would be a factor. However, if his amnesia regarding his actions is real and not just due to alcohol, that would suggest that he himself cannot accept his own perverse violent potential. Alcohol may be needed for him to express that side of himself, and the ability to forget about it later, by repressing memories, further protects him from coming face to face with the person he has been. Of course, it is quite possible, perhaps likely, that Grant remembers much more of Kathryn's killing than he is willing to say. In that case, if there were other killings before hers, he would also remember them.

To understand why I was so concerned about whether Grant might have been a serial sadistic murderer, let me describe the features often seen in sadistic killers in general and compare them with Grant's history. I believe there are sufficient similarities in this description to worry about Grant having been or becoming a serial killer.

The sadistic killer is almost always male. He is the one who makes the hairs on the back of your neck stand up as you listen to his story, if he is willing to tell it. In the absence of a confession, reading the evidence gathered by police is sufficient to produce a similar reaction. Sadistic murder is motivated by the thrill of causing pain, suffering and death. Part of that thrill is usually sexual, with rape or sexual degradation being involved. The rape may occur after the killing, and it is then called necrophilia. Sometimes there is no sexual assault but just exerting power, and inflicting violence and humiliation that produces the thrill. Some of the other possible thrills are the stuff of nightmares, like feeding on human flesh, or the gruesome mutilation of a corpse.

Sadistic killings don't come out of the blue fully formed. They will have been the subject of developing and detailed fantasy by the killer for years beforehand. He will have rehearsed his actions in detail in his mind—and masturbated to them—developing what the police will call his modus operandi. When the event actually occurs, he will be playing out that fantasy in real life and he will want it to go perfectly to script. If it isn't right, he will do it again to get it right. Having done it, the drive will go away for a while but then start to build up until he has to do it again.

A sadistic killer prepares and acts in secret. Outwardly, he is likely to be leading an apparently normal life. Family members, neighbours and workmates may have no idea who they are dealing with. But inwardly, he is anything but normal. He usually has significant psychopathic traits, with no empathy for his eventual victims; his sexuality is bizarre; and he is driven by his strong sexual deviancy or need to inflict pain. Once he is caught, it may be obvious that there were warning signs. But who among us suspects a serial killer in our midst? A sadistic killer is most commonly a lone wolf, but there are times when he is assisted by a partner, usually a troubled, dependent woman who is drawn into the murder as an accomplice or facilitator. She may actually be similarly disordered and perverse but unlikely to get involved in such gruesome matters on her own.

In Grant's case, I was particularly concerned that the methodical way in which Kathryn's murder was carried out suggested he had practised before. To go from fantasy to such an efficient and complex offence in one step would, I thought, be unusual. Also, the fact that he kept Kathryn's clothing and put it with other female clothing in his bag was strongly suggestive of an attachment to these trophies for use in future sexual fantasy. It showed a level of confidence that he would not be caught, perhaps because he had got away with other murders before this. The little sketch map with the stick figure was also very suspicious. Killers may wish to return to the scene of the crime to re-experience the sexual thrill. All of this led me to think that Grant's reported poor memory might not be genuine.

Grant's killing was driven by powerful perverse sexual drives. Whatever the background factors in his earlier life actually were, they produced a severe personality disorder with psychopathic traits that meant his controls over his killer instinct were defective from the start. Alcoholic intoxication was used to further reduce any lingering inhibitions. We will presumably never know the full story, as Grant is unlikely to reveal it. But at least now he is unable to do it all again.

3

AN OBSESSIONAL MAN

At 7.30 a.m. on a Wednesday in June 1997, 47-year-old Peter Lock answered his home phone. It was his daughter Susan calling from London, where she lived. Peter greeted her and asked how she was. Susan said she was fine and asked if she could speak to her mother, Gay, to follow up on something they'd spoken about a few days earlier. Her father, who sounded bright and breezy, said that Gay was still asleep. He suggested Susan call back in ten minutes, giving him time to rouse her mother. Susan called back as suggested only to find her father agitated and distraught. He told Susan that when he'd gone into her mother's room to wake her, he'd found she had apparently been attacked by an intruder. There was lots of blood and he feared she was 'gone'. Peter told his shocked daughter that he had to hang up so that he could call triple zero.

Ambulance and police officers attended soon after Peter Lock's emergency call. They found Gay Lock, aged forty-six, in the bedroom she occupied separately from her husband. She had a deeply depressed fracture of her skull, and there was a lot of blood spatter and pooling around her pillow and bedding. It was immediately evident that she had been dead for at least several hours. There did not appear to be evidence of a struggle—it looked as if Gay had been struck while sleeping. Peter told police he was a heavy sleeper and he had heard nothing. He said it was a little unusual for Gay to sleep beyond 7 a.m., but he'd thought nothing of it when she hadn't stirred that morning, and she generally didn't like to be disturbed in her room.

Police did find evidence that suggested there had been a break-in. There was a ladder up against the front of the house, and an upstairs windowpane had been broken to gain access. Some drawers in Gay's room had been left open. Police at first wondered whether a burglar might not have realised the room was occupied and, when Gay stirred, they panicked and hit her on the head. However, they soon found that things didn't add up. The window that had apparently been used to gain entry had been broken from the inside, as the glass fragments were mainly outside on the roof. There were no fingerprints anywhere. Nothing was identified as missing from the house.

Furthermore, the injury to Gay appeared to have been made by a very heavy object shaped like the head of a hammer, but a thorough search had found no such weapon. Peter said he owned two hammers, but police only found one small one in his shed. He was uncertain about the location of the other larger hammer.

Suspicion fell upon Peter. He was interviewed a number of times over the next three days, but each time he stuck to his story. Police suggested he take a lie-detector test—probably a bluff, because that evidence is not used in Australian courts—but Peter refused, saying it was not necessary: he was telling the truth and they should believe him. Then, four days after the murder, Peter appeared at the police station. He was agitated and hyperventilating. He refused to actually speak but wrote a confession to the murder of his wife, whereupon he was taken into custody.

For the next week, Peter remained completely mute, refusing to speak at all. But, strangely, he communicated copiously in writing. He wrote long accounts of his actions, describing in detail the issues that had led him to act in the way he had. He eventually explained, on paper, that for years he had lied to people, especially to Gay, covering up his omissions and shortcomings—he would go on to say that his lying to Gay was the main reason for her death. He believed he lied impulsively when he spoke and that it was far less likely that he would lie if he wrote out what he wanted to say. The very act of having to think about what he wanted to communicate in writing stopped him from lying. Therefore, he had decided to only write, rather than speak, until he had given a full account of the truth.

After Peter had begun to speak again, he was sent to prison on remand for murder. It was there he was seen for psychiatric assessment and court reports on behalf of his defence lawyers, and later by psychiatrists appointed by the court. I saw him in that capacity seventeen months after Gay's death.

When I assessed Peter in prison, he was pleasant and cooperative. He was rather discursive in his speaking style, but other than that his thought processes were normal, though he was a bit teary at times. He had been interviewed by another psychiatrist a week earlier and that had left him feeling emotionally unsettled. All the memories and sadness he had been trying to contain had been stirred up. His recall of the days leading up to the murder was a bit patchy by that time, but he clearly remembered his denial of guilt for three days after the crime, then saying over and over to himself, 'I killed Gay, and they know it.'

Peter told me that he had planned the murder on the Sunday prior to the act and gone to elaborate lengths to set the scene. On the Tuesday afternoon he'd organised a breakdown of his vehicle in the car park at work, removing a part from the engine so that the car wouldn't start—he didn't want a car to be parked outside his house, so that it could be surmised a potential intruder would think there was no-one home. He even called roadside assistance so that there would be evidence of the breakdown. After the mechanic told him someone had tampered with his car and they'd need to get a spare part the next day, Peter caught a taxi home. The night before the killing, Peter went to his shed and removed the larger of his two hammers, which he hid in his bedroom. Then, in the early hours of Wednesday morning, Peter quietly went into Gay's room, where she was deeply asleep, and struck a single heavy blow to her head with the hammer, the head of which almost buried itself in her skull. To his consternation, Gay didn't die immediately. Peter lay on top of her for some minutes until she stopped twitching and jerking.

Having killed Gay, Peter set about making it appear that there'd been an intruder. He went downstairs and, after making sure no neighbours were about, got his ladder from the garage—which was so cluttered there was no room for the car—and placed it up against the eave nearest the upstairs hallway window. Then he smashed the window where the intruder would have entered. He went back to Gay's room and, making sure not to leave fingerprints, opened a couple of drawers and moved some things around, like a burglar looking for valuables. He didn't linger in there, and he tried not to look at Gay's lifeless body. Lastly, he crossed the backyard of his house into adjoining bushland, where he threw the hammer as far as he could into dense undergrowth—it was never found.

During the actual killing, Peter felt like a robot. He was detached from his actions, cut off from his feelings, going through the motions of murder without the emotions he thought he should have. It was as if, at that time, he had split in two, with one part coolly carrying out the killing of his wife, and the other part observing with horror yet unable to stop what was happening. However, afterwards, despite his strange detachment at the time, he was able to fully recall the details of what he had done.

Peter felt that he and Gay had been relating quite well in the weeks leading up to the murder. They had separate rooms but they liked to get together for sex a few times each weekend, and had done so on the Sunday prior. They had also been seeing friends and attending a weekly prayer group. Peter even recalled the pleasure he had felt as Gay enthusiastically related to him the details of a long telephone conversation she had had with a friend on the Tuesday. But he explained that he had a certain kind of personality that had led to major distortions in his relationship with his wife. A variety of stressors had led to increasing tension in him, and between him and his wife, eventually culminating in his decision to kill her.

Gay was about to discover a long history of dishonesty and incompetence that he had managed to keep from her. In his mind, the most serious deceit was that for twelve years he had not submitted tax returns on her behalf, when she was under the impression that he had. He had hidden his ineptitude by using a secret post office box for all tax department correspondence. But recently, Gay had been putting pressure on him to use a tax agent for the returns. He knew that if he did, the truth would be revealed and he wouldn't be able to cope with her rage and distress.

Peter described his own personality in detail in his writings. It was evident that he'd given this a great deal of thought. He had very strong obsessional traits. He set very high standards for himself in terms of his own performance. He was excessively tidy and meticulous, checking things repeatedly to make sure he'd made no mistakes. He also had an enormous need to be loved and approved of by others, particularly by Gay—he hated conflict and would do anything to avoid it. However, despite his high standards, Peter was actually inefficient and incompetent. He made endless lists and plans but rarely saw things though to completion.

Early in his marriage, Peter's inefficiencies had caused considerable conflict, which had been noticed by various friends. Gay was herself a demanding and obsessional person who became very distressed if Peter failed to carry out tasks properly. He found her extreme disappointment too much to cope with, so he established a pattern in their relationship where he consistently lied about what he had done. By covering up his failures, he had kept the peace. Over the years, Gay had mellowed; she'd become less demanding, less of a perfectionist. Nevertheless, Peter was convinced that if she found out about his deception, she would be extremely angry and upset. He found it impossible to contemplate the consequences.

A range of other stressors had built up and contributed to Peter's actions. Over the last couple of years, Gay had lost both her parents as well as her brother. Peter had been the executor of his father-in-law's will and found this a very trying task. Gay had also had surgery for uterine cancer during those years. At Peter's workplace, the Worldwide Church of God, there had been some restructuring and two key workers had been laid off, so Peter's workload had increased. He'd been assigned to redesign the computer system, a task he found impossible—only months before the killing, the church had lost five years' worth of invaluable data. There seemed to be a loss of corporate direction too, with long-term, dedicated staff being treated poorly. Peter feared he might lose his job. All this was very difficult for an obsessional man to deal with.

In retrospect, there had been ominous warnings of what was to come. For some years, Peter had from time to time experienced the thought that it would be better for both Gay and himself if she were to die. He used to fantasise that she would die in a tragic accident or from some incurable illness. Then he would be able to sort out all the tasks that he could not finish while she was alive. However, he did not see himself as the agent of Gay's death until shortly before her murder.

Peter even managed to convince himself that Gay was willing or ready to die. She had, after all, talked about having done everything she wanted to achieve in her life, and being ready to move on. She had also discussed possible funeral arrangements. The main reason she didn't want to die was the thought that Peter might marry some-one else. On his part, Peter had told Gay that he wasn't ready to die, as there were things that he still had to do—in an oblique way, he was trying to tell Gay about his many unfinished tasks, but he wasn't explicit enough for her to really understand what he meant.

A recurring theme of death by hammer blow may have been another important sign. Peter had experienced over several years dreams in which he would be struck over the head with a hammer. He would wake from those dreams in a state of distress, puzzled about what they might mean. Later, he could not work out whether they had anything to do with what he did to Gay. Also, a year before the murder, when a stray cat had been bothering the couple, Peter had taken it into the nearby bushland and killed it by striking it on the head with the same hammer he later used to kill Gay—she had actually suggested he do this. He had found it repugnant at the time but, perhaps in a strange way, his action, and Gay's suggestion he do it, might have played some role in his later formulation of the murder plan.

I was keen to explore how Peter had been functioning in the months before the murder, to see if there was evidence of any significant mental illness developing. Peter believed that, despite all the stressors he had outlined, he had actually managed quite well in that time. The one problem he had was with sleep. There was not one night in the last six months when he had had more than three hours sleep. He would often slumber for one or two hours and then be fully awake, so he would get up and work on his computer. Peter attributed the problem to 'oxygen drops', a mysterious naturopathic therapy—he had no idea what the drops actually contained—that Gay had used since her hysterectomy. They'd seemed to help her so much that he'd decided to take them too. He found they gave him 'boundless' energy, despite his lack of sleep, although every now and then he would suddenly get very fatigued and this would last a few days until his energy rebounded again.

Peter's mood had been generally positive. In the evening he might be a bit despondent if he hadn't achieved his aims for the day, but he unwound by talking to Gay and watching some television. The only evidence of depression was an occasional period of two or three days when he would feel 'blue'—Peter had felt like this in the days leading up the murder—which he couldn't tell Gay about because it stemmed from the burden of his deceit. But he never got depressed to the point of feeling suicidal. After he had been withdrawn for a few days, Gay would admonish him and he would pull himself out of it. Peter had never had longer periods of depression and definitely no psychotic symptoms, such as delusions or hallucinations. He had never had to seek medical or psychiatric treatment for any mental illness.

The robotic state Peter described at the time of the murder was, from his description, a state of depersonalisation. This is a mild form of dissociation commonly used by the mind to cut off feelings at times of intense stress or emotion. It is a protective mechanism that can occur in normal people who are under stress or feeling anxious, or as a symptom of depression or psychosis.

After the murder, Peter was 'putting on an act' of being a distressed victim, but in a way his grief was genuine. After a few days, the full realisation of what he had done hit home and he entered a state of mutism. In many instances, sudden mutism is a symptom of severe depression or psychosis, but it can be voluntary. In Peter's case, he had not shown significant mental illness prior to the murder and the mutism seems to have been motivated entirely by his grief about and remorse for his actions, and his need to be entirely honest. Over subsequent months, Peter showed symptoms of post-traumatic stress. He had nightmares about the murder and flashbacks, and episodes of severe distress and tearfulness. When I saw him, seventeen months after the murder, he was still intermittently upset.

Generally, Peter's medical history was unremarkable except for suffering from asthma since the age of eighteen, which was mostly managed through use of the usual inhalers. But about a year before the murder he had a more severe episode requiring oral steroid medication, and this produced 'extreme behavioural changes'. He became secretive and odd—he started writing four books on unusual subjects. After ten days, Gay told him to stop taking the steroids because he was becoming 'dangerous', though no actual aggression was reported. Once he'd stopped, he quickly returned to normal. If only Gay had realised how dangerous her husband could really be.

Peter's parents were alive and well. His father was a commercial artist who later became involved in various wholesale businesses. He was helpful to other people, sometimes to the extent that he neglected his own family. Peter understood that his father had been discharged from army service in his younger years for some kind of nervous disorder, and he used to joke to Susan: 'If I ever get like Dad was, take me out and hit me over the head with a hammer.' Peter's mother was a retired art teacher who was anxious, hated loud noise and didn't always cope well with her children, but she'd never had any psychiatric treatment. Peter was the eldest of four siblings. His brother was a high school teacher, married with two children. One sister, divorced with one child, was 'unusual, bohemian and artistic' and occasionally taught art. The other sister had 'never grown up' and had recently separated from her husband. One of Peter's nephews had been diagnosed with schizophrenia.

Peter was a bright and motivated student at school, and an avid reader, but he constantly sought approval. At age twelve, Peter was sexually propositioned by his scoutmaster, but he managed to get away before anything significant occurred. In his adult life Peter had briefly worked in insurance, but for many years he worked in an administrative role for the Worldwide Church of God. He and Gay had married when they were both twenty-three, and had the one daughter. There was no history of any legal offences, but Peter had been fined once for failing to lodge a tax return. He never touched illicit drugs and never abused alcohol, only enjoying one or two beers from time to time. At one stage he had secretly gambled but then forced himself to stop before he was discovered.

Peter's case initially went to Queensland's Mental Health Court. He did not deny killing Gay, or even the fact that he had planned it for at least three days, but his lawyers sought a psychiatric defence of either unsoundness of mind or diminished responsibility. No fewer than five psychiatrists and one psychologist assessed him, either at his lawyer's request or by the order of the court. There was a fair divergence of opinion among them.

The three psychiatrists who saw him for the defence all agreed Peter had an obsessional personality. All considered that he also had an adjustment disorder at the time, with symptoms of anxiety and some depression. One went so far as to make a diagnosis of a brief psychotic disorder that might have been present for only minutes or even seconds at the time of the killing. That diagnosis seemed to have been made on the basis of the depersonalisation and apparently inexplicable, out-of-character nature of Peter's behaviour in killing Gay, but under cross-examination it did not hold up.

The two psychiatrists who gave evidence at the order of the court (one of whom was me) agreed with the obsessional personality view, and thought it was possibly combined with some passive-aggressive traits. However, we found insufficient evidence of mental illness, over and above the obsessionality and some mild anxiety and mood instability, to make a diagnosis of any mental disorder sufficient for a psychiatric defence.

The Mental Health Court made a finding of no defence and fit for trial. Peter took the matter to the mainstream Supreme Court for a trial before a jury, but the jury could not come to a decision, so a second trial was held. This time a different jury found Peter guilty of murder and he was sentenced to life in prison. Peter's lawyers mounted an appeal, which was granted on the basis that the trial judge had failed to provide the jury with an adequate summing up of the evidence. Because of the judge's failings, the jury was left with inadequate guidance to be able to navigate their way through the complex and diverse expert evidence. Had they had proper instructions, they might have reached the same verdict, or might have found for either unsoundness (probably unlikely) or diminished responsibility. Therefore, the verdict was found to be unsafe and a third trial was ordered.

The new jury was provided with evidence from a psychiatrist that persuaded them that Peter had been suffering from a degree of anxiety and depression prior to the murder such as to substantially impair his judgement at that time. A finding of not guilty of murder was made, but Peter was found guilty of manslaughter on the basis of diminished responsibility. The judge then sentenced him to six years imprisonment.

What can we make of this crime, committed by a man with no history of violence?

Peter had a dysfunctional personality. He was markedly obsessional, with a strong need for control and organisation in his life. At the same time, he was paradoxically inefficient. His obsessionality had gone beyond being a useful trait, as it can be, and become a liability. He also had a powerful need for approval from others, Gay in particular, and a need to perform to his own very high expectations. He was acutely aware of being afraid of Gay's disapproval, but he had very little awareness of any anger—he had almost no ability to express that emotion, having avoided conflict all his life. It is likely that deep down he was angry that Gay would be disappointed in him when she discovered his failings regarding the tax returns. With the pressure building at work and at home, he'd fantasised an escape through Gay's death. Hammer blows came in his dreams, blows that Gay had approved when she instructed him to kill the stray cat.

Obsessional defences help to keep emotional conflicts buried and controlled, which is helpful up to a point. But when the pressure a person is feeling rises, those defences can eventually give way and, when they do, the results can be devastating. Emotions can explode, with the source of the pressure being targeted. In Peter's case, it was a controlled and rationalised explosion: a pre-emptive strike. He was able to make himself believe that Gay's death was more palatable than the dreaded loss of approval and self-esteem. These very unusual and disturbed thought patterns arose out of Peter's personality rather than any significant mental illness.

I have seen a small number of cases over the years where obsessional defences have given way, with murder the result. However, in those cases the provocations were much more obvious and severe. In Peter's case, an external view of the provocations would not justify the actions he took. They are only understandable if one tries

to understand Peter's conflicted inner world and the priorities that
held sway for him. Obsessional personality traits do not usually lead
to violence; on the contrary, they usually militate against aggression.
But in Peter's case, it appears, his fear of failure in Gay's eyes and
potential rejection by her provoked him to drastic action.

There is the possibility that other factors were at play that Peter
did not reveal to the police or to any of the assessing psychiatrists.
Those factors could mean that the murder of Gay was a much more
calculated act than he let on, and that his elaborate written explanations were designed to hide the real truth.

A long time after my involvement in this case, I came upon a
newsletter from the Worldwide Church of God, Peter's one-time
employer. It had a section describing the distress the murder had caused
within the church and raising various possibilities regarding motive.

The church was a Sabbatarian (Sunday-worshipping) sect that
originated in the United States as a breakaway from the more
mainstream Seventh-day Adventists, who celebrate the sabbath on
Saturday. After the death of its charismatic leader, it was riven by
theological disagreements and power struggles, leading to a split
into two rival subgroups—one representing the old guard and the
other dissenters—with much ill feeling between them. The newsletter suggested that Gay Lock had joined the dissenting group,
whereas Peter had stuck with the status quo. It further suggested
that Gay attended separate prayer groups with her faction, and that
no-one from the church's hierarchy attended her funeral. Some in
the church believed that Peter had killed Gay as a misguided act of
faith, doing what he believed was God's will, while others alleged
that Gay had left Peter on a few occasions and that her killing was
an act of vengeful rage by him. Some hoped that, in fact, Gay had
been suffering from cancer and that the murder was a mercy killing.
Yet another theory was that Peter had his eye on another woman in
the church and had planned to be the sad widower in order to start
a relationship with her. Ironically, years earlier he had been featured
in the church magazine describing the secrets to a happy marriage.

All of this was very different from the story told to me by Peter. These various theories might well just be a search for meaning by members of the church who used their imaginations to explain something terrible that happened in their midst. Peter is perhaps the only one who knows the truth—although, given the complexities of his psychological make-up, even he may be in the dark.

If Peter's explanations of his crime are accepted, Gay's murder can best be seen as an unusual kind of defensive murder. In most such murders, the situations bringing them about are more readily understood than in this case.

Most people will be familiar with the 'fight or flight' phenomenon in that, when confronted with a threat, we experience fear, or at least a sense of facing a challenge. The sympathetic nervous system lights up and our heart races, our breathing accelerates, and our circulation adjusts to enable us to react effectively, either by running away or standing our ground. We have inherited this response from our evolutionary forebears, who faced a lot of challenges to their survival on a daily basis. Our response to such a state of arousal is affected by all kinds of factors, such as our parenting, the models we have seen or learned, and our ability to solve problems and make decisions under stress. It is also dependent on the integrity of the areas of the brain that control our emotions and tell us how best to react. If those areas are not functioning normally, because of disease or the temporary effects of intoxication, we may overreact and respond with far more aggression than is necessary. Everything can happen so quickly that we fail to control ourselves. That may result in murder.

Sometimes the threat will be so severe and sudden that we have no choice but to react to save our own life. Examples could include a policeman being attacked or a householder coming across an intruder who turns on them. Such scenarios might allow us a legal argument of self-defence, in which case a killing is not classified as murder. If the external threat is severe and recurrent but not immediate, it may nevertheless sometimes be seen as a threat sufficient to justify killing in self-defence. An example is the so-called 'battered wife syndrome'. The traumatised offender may be exonerated or get the lesser conviction of manslaughter. Peter's explanation might be seen as one such slow-burning response to a pending threat.

My objective assessment struggled to see the external threat in the very severe light that it seems to have presented to Peter. His inner turmoil and sense of doom appeared to arise from strong, largely suppressed emotions and defects in his self-esteem rather than the external reality of the situation. However, he was able to persuade a jury that he had sufficient abnormality of mind to produce a defence of diminished responsibility, and that saved him from a life sentence.

By its very nature, defensive murder is generally a once-only offence committed in unique circumstances. That means Peter is unlikely to kill again—unless, of course, his motives were much colder and more calculated than he says.

4

AN URGE TO KILL

On an autumn night in 2010, just before midnight, an ambulance arrived at a home in one of Brisbane's older suburbs, where 21-year-old Rhys Austin lived with his parents and three brothers. The whole family was standing in the driveway. The father and one boy were bending over a young female lying on the ground, performing CPR on her. The youngest son looked terrified, shrinking back into the shadows, a hand to his mouth. The mother had her arms around her second son, Rhys. He was staring wide-eyed at the motionless form of his girlfriend, Bianca Girven.

As the ambulance officers took over the resuscitation, they were told that some assailants had strangled Bianca. At first no pulse could be found, but the officers managed after a few minutes of work and high-flow oxygen to restore a weak circulation and whisked Bianca away to the nearby Princess Alexandra Hospital. There, she was put on life support, but by late the next day, tests showed her to be brain-dead and the machines were turned off. The post-mortem confirmed death from asphyxia (lack of oxygen)—there were compression injuries to Bianca's neck. She was just twenty-two years old, and mother to a three-year-old son from another relationship. Her family was devastated.

Police made some preliminary inquiries at the scene and then took Rhys to the station, where they interviewed him for several hours. He told them that, after attending the Full Moon Fire Spinning Festival beside the Brisbane River at West End, he and Bianca had gone to nearby Mount Gravatt, the feature whose name was given to the surrounding leafy suburb. At a car park on the mountain that was popular with couples, they talked for a while and then had a cuddle, with sex on their minds, in the back of the family van that Rhys was using that night. Suddenly, the van's sliding door was thrown open and someone reached in, struck Bianca and then dragged her out of the vehicle. Rhys said that he went to Bianca's aid but was struck on the head by another person and fell headfirst onto the bitumen. He was ordered to stay on the ground, where, confused and scared, he heard gurgling and choking noises. An assailant took his phone from his pocket and smashed it on the ground; then things went quiet. When Rhys finally got up, he found Bianca lying there, unconscious. He couldn't feel a pulse and in a panic he tried some CPR, but Bianca didn't respond. With his phone destroyed, and desperate to get some help, Rhys hauled Bianca's body into the van and drove down the mountain to his parents' home. He said he had no idea who the two assailants were, or why he and Bianca had been targeted.

The police made extensive inquiries. They were suspicious about the truthfulness of Rhys's account from the start, but there was no doubt Rhys had injuries to his face and his phone was smashed. It was four months later that they arrested Rhys and charged him with Bianca's murder. Despite this, for another next ten months from his arrest, Rhys maintained his story.

Within days of Bianca's death, Rhys had voluntarily admitted himself to the mental health service at Princess Alexandra Hospital for grief counselling, saying that he felt unsafe in the community. He was well known to hospital staff as a diagnosed schizophrenic and had been in community treatment when Bianca was attacked. Later, after being charged, Rhys was remanded in custody at the high-security Arthur Gorrie Correctional Centre in Wacol. But his mental condition caused concern, so he was transferred to the nearby High Secure Inpatient Service at The Park Hospital for better observation and assessment. He was initially assessed by his treating psychiatrist as a man with a known psychosis: a self-reported grieving victim of crime, but one who might be playing on his symptoms to get out of jail and into the more comfortable environment of the hospital.

Rhys finally opened up about Bianca's murder to another psychiatrist, who saw him to prepare a forensic report for the court. He admitted killing Bianca, describing a complex set of delusional beliefs and psychotic experiences that he said led him to carry out the act. However, he did not believe he had a mental illness. The killing was, in his mind, necessary and justified. Everything he revealed had been real to him at the time of the murder and remained just as real fourteen months later.

Six months after his admission to the forensic hospital, I saw Rhys at the order of the Mental Health Court to report on his diagnosis and provide my opinion on the issues of unsoundness of mind, diminished responsibility, fitness for trial, and treatment needs in the context of future risk. Assessments and reports had been conducted by two psychiatrists at the request of the defence, his treating psychiatrists provided reports, and I was one of two further psychiatrists appointed by the court to provide independent reports. For the first three hours of our interview his account stayed the same, but over the following two hours he really opened up. It became evident that he was very good at hiding the full extent of his delusional inner world from outside scrutiny. It took a very long interview to break through the secrecy and communication barriers. What he revealed was very disturbing.

Rhys's mental health problems started in 2005 when he was just sixteen, triggered by considerable drug abuse. Up until that age he had been a normal boy: popular at school, good at sport, form captain in Grade 11. But with the development of a mental illness, he floundered. His university studies went unfinished, and he wafted from one temporary job to another. There was a family history of mental illness. Rhys's paternal grandfather had been admitted years earlier to a mental hospital with a psychotic illness, and he'd remained there until he died. Other members of his father's extended family had depression, and one cousin had attempted suicide. This seemed to indicate some inherited vulnerability to mental illness in Rhys, exacerbated by the use of drugs.

Rhys had used just about every illicit drug available, accompanied by alcohol. He started with marijuana but it didn't suit him. It prompted disordered thoughts and some odd beliefs about telepathic communication, and he became withdrawn. So he moved on to ecstasy at parties. He tried LSD a handful of times and it caused spectacular hallucinations. He flirted with speed and ice, which made him hyperactive and disinhibited. He intermittently used heroin and crushed-up oxycodone, a strong opioid painkiller also known on the streets as 'hippy heroin'. He even tried inhaling nitrous oxide in combination with ecstasy, which caused him to black out a few times. His use of these substances was modified over time, because in treating his mental illness, his doctors recommended he stop using drugs—although from time to time he would still take something. However, he wasn't on drugs at the time of the murder.

Due to his mental illness, Rhys's thinking and behaviour were disturbed: he started hearing voices and he became withdrawn. He cut himself with a knife or a razor a few times. When he was admitted to a private psychiatric clinic, nurses reported worrying behaviour: Rhys carried a knife, had a sexual relationship with another patient, and was found lying on the floor of female patients' rooms or standing in the dark at their doors. He seemed to improve after being given antipsychotic and antidepressant medication and was discharged after a few weeks, but several months later the problems returned and he was readmitted. After just one night, Rhys absconded, and it was decided he couldn't be managed in the private setting. He was transferred to the psychiatric unit of the regional general hospital, where antipsychotics were continued and there was a confirmed diagnosis of schizophrenia, triggered by drug abuse.

All up, Rhys had a half-dozen admissions to the psychiatric unit over three years. Treatment was frustratingly difficult as he seemed not to respond very well to anything, despite the gamut of antipsychotics available (by the time of Bianca's murder, he was taking his prescribed medication only occasionally). The emphasis of treatment shifted to supportive psychotherapy, giving Rhys strategies to cope with his symptoms, since it seemed impossible to remove them with medication. The voices and other symptoms were always there, but he didn't talk as much about them and at times seemed more settled.

However, things weren't as settled as superficially they may have seemed—several times over the years, Rhys had come close to killing someone. He didn't tell anyone about most of those occasions, and those that were known were not given the significance they deserved, at least when looked at retrospectively. Had they been fully understood in terms of the thinking driving them, not just the actions themselves, they might have been recognised as a red flag warning of a possible future murder.

Rhys told me that he'd first started having urges to kill people in about 2006. It was all part of his delusional thinking and a response to the voices he was hearing. At first, he couldn't really work out was happening. He had a confused awareness that some kind of 'entity' was taking control of his mind. The entity communicated with him via at least one male voice, which, firmly and insistently, talked about killing someone. Rhys came to believe over time that he needed to kill in order to demonstrate that he could do it and thereby please the entity. He thought he had become a special person, with special abilities, chosen for a special task. He realised that the entity was some kind of god. Later, he saw that god as some kind of all-powerful computer that could place radio waves in his mind.

As his illness progressed, he began to believe that he could communicate telepathically with others. By this means, he had communicated with family, friends, even some famous people. However, those others would never talk openly, with their real voices, about what had been said telepathically. He also became aware of messages that came to him via the television or radio. He would hear a statement or a song and recognise its particular significance to him alone; instructions would also come by that means. He realised he could use his mind in ways that others couldn't, and that there was some role he had to play in the future that would be important for the world.

In addition to the voices, which he usually heard when he was quiet and not distracted, Rhys had occasional visual and olfactory hallucinations. He would see fleeting movements of light and shadows, but would generally know they weren't real. In the earlier stages of his illness, he also at times smelled a powerful odour for which there was no source—of 'poo, body odour, perfume or marijuana'.

All of these experiences became more prominent when Rhys smoked pot or used LSD or speed. The drugs triggered the earliest experiences, but then they progressed on their own, even when he wasn't using anything.

Despite the strangeness of these beliefs and experiences, Rhys did not see them as caused by an illness. Many doctors and nurses told him they were, but he didn't believe them. What he experienced was, for him, powerful, personal and real. He knew that the treatment was designed to make these things go away, but he didn't see the need for that to happen. In any case, the medication wasn't effective in stopping the experiences, although it did dampen them down a little. He saw little need to take the tablets and didn't do so when not under involuntary treatment. He looked at other patients in the hospital and he could see that they were not well, but he was different.

In general, Rhys did not talk to his therapists about his experiences. He would admit to voices and other symptoms but tended to minimise his accounts, and he never talked freely about the extent of his urges to kill. He was aware that most people, especially his doctors, would regard these things as abnormal. He was especially careful about saying anything to his family, as he knew they would worry and might send him back to hospital. In any case, he could converse with them telepathically.

I encouraged Rhys to tell me about all the episodes prior to Bianca's murder where he had come close to killing someone. The first one he remembered occurred in 2006. He was at home and the entity's voice was insistent, so in the middle of the night he went for a walk up Mount Gravatt, the voice telling him what he should do as he climbed. At the summit, he picked up a large stick that he thought would be a suitable weapon with which to kill somebody. He saw some people sitting in their cars, and he went up to one vehicle and tapped on the window. But he was seized with sudden ambivalence and doubt, and instead of killing the occupant, he asked for a cigarette and walked away. He regretted not carrying out the deed, but he told himself there would be another chance soon and went home to bed.

About two months later, a schoolmate was staying over. They had been hanging out and smoking pot together. They'd both gone to bed, in separate rooms, when Rhys had the strong impulse to kill his friend. He picked up a cricket stump, went into his friend's room, and raised the stump over the sleeping boy. Once again he was frozen with doubt, and he went back to bed.

A similar thing happened when he went on a meditation weekend. He ran away from the camp after stealing a knife from the kitchen. He was about to catch a train when he saw a campervan near the station and heard the instruction to go and kill the occupants. When he approached the van, the old couple inside offered him a cup of tea. He sat with them for a while, consumed by the thought that he should stab them, but instead he asked them about the train timetable and left, again full of regrets. On yet another occasion, Rhys went into a suburban house at night, planning to kill the residents, but once again his courage failed him. With each failed attempt, however, his desire to kill seemed to grow stronger: he had to show the god-voice that he could do it.

He came even closer the next time. It was 2008 and Rhys and Bianca had started seeing each other again after previous efforts had turned sour. As they were walking down a road, Rhys's thoughts and the voices in his head were pressing. He took out a small blade, held Bianca tight, and put the blade to her throat, cutting her slightly. Suddenly, he froze. He felt 'awkward'. Bianca managed to take the blade and talked to Rhys while she walked him to her mother's house nearby. There, she phoned Rhys's parents and told them what had happened. They came over immediately and took him straight to hospital.

Rhys hadn't given much thought to what would have happened had he succeeded in cutting Bianca's throat. He'd had some vague notion that he might go to jail, but that seemed unimportant. The fact that he might have succeeded meant far more than the consequences for his life. He seemed not to have thought about Bianca or her family.

At that point, the violence was clearly escalating. Later, at trial, it was disturbing to hear the evidence of the psychiatrist who'd treated Rhys after the murder. She'd been unaware of the knife attack on Bianca. Somewhere, somehow, communication of these important facts did not occur.

While he was in hospital after assaulting Bianca, Rhys shared a room with another patient, who was pleasant and friendly. That man was not aware, nor were the staff, that Rhys was still having disturbing thoughts. His medication had been changed and the voices were now more prominent; he was also seeing strange images that others could not see. One evening Rhys thought he heard his roommate say nasty things about his family, and he had an overpowering urge to kill the man. While the man slept, Rhys got a towel, wet it, and rolled it up. He then put the towel around the man's neck and pulled it tight. The man woke up to find himself being strangled.

He struggled violently and, with great effort, dragged himself into the corridor, where he screamed for help. Staff and security officers responded and Rhys was placed in isolation. Rhys later recalled thinking, 'Oh shit, I shouldn't be doing this', but at the same time he wished he'd succeeded in killing someone.

The facts of this assault should, by rights, have earned Rhys a charge of attempted murder. However, police seemed to be heavily influenced by the fact that the incident happened in a psychiatric ward and the victim was not keen to press charges. It was listed as a lowly common assault. It is a sad irony that the hearing of that charge was delayed repeatedly because of Rhys's poor mental health and, when finally heard, it was in conjunction with another charge—the murder of Bianca. The knife assault on Bianca and the attack on a fellow patient were events that signalled Rhys's murderous potential, but these warnings were not heeded or perhaps even recognised for what they were, and the tragic consequence was a young woman's death.

After the incident with the blade, Rhys and Bianca broke up again. However, in 2009 Rhys contacted her and they started seeing each other yet again. They'd had a long, intermittent relationship. Bianca had been Rhys's first sexual partner, at the age of fourteen. By the time 2009 rolled around, Bianca had been through a brief marriage to and divorce from a Balinese man and had a young son. She lived with her parents and her sister, all of whom Rhys got on well with.

The night before Bianca's murder, Rhys stayed over at her house and they had sex. Things seemed quite good between them. But for the past few days Rhys had been hearing voices again and having a lot of thoughts about killing Bianca, as well as about possibly killing himself too. He'd also begun to believe that he was communicating with Bianca telepathically, talking to her about preparing herself for death, and that she was telling him she would try to do so. At the same time he was feeling suspicious and thought people might be listening to or watching him.

On the fateful day, Rhys was due to go to a university class on creative writing, but at the last minute he decided to go and see Bianca instead. He then impulsively jumped on and off a series of buses, buying things as he went: some movies from a video store; a wooden chest costing $180 (purchased on lay-by); some beer; and two bottles of cough syrup because he'd heard it could get you high. Back on a bus, Rhys phoned Bianca and they arranged to meet at her local shops, before heading back to Bianca's place to hang out. Throughout all this erratic behaviour, Rhys felt more and more stressed, the telepathic conversation with Bianca flowing unbroken.

At the Full Moon Fire Spinning Festival that evening, they watched some fire twirling and other events, and Rhys later recalled that it was 'romantic and very nice'. Later, they returned to Mount Gravatt—Rhys had decided that he needed to take Bianca somewhere so that he could tell her some 'special things', which he believed he'd flagged with her telepathically. (He was unable to explain during our interview exactly what these special things were, though, beyond 'voices and stuff'.) At the mountain's uppermost car park, where they spent a little time looking at the city lights, Rhys felt awkward and unsettled—there were too many people around for him to speak to Bianca about the special things. So they drove down to the lower car park, where they found themselves alone. Rhys's mind was full of the fact that he had to kill Bianca, but he recalled his previous failures to follow through. He knew he had to try harder to fulfil his destiny this time.

They chatted for a while on the front seat of the van, then Rhys suggested they get into the back, where they could lie down. Perhaps Bianca thought they would have sex. On any other night that would have been a possibility, but not on this night. Rhys asked Bianca if she'd ever experienced voices in her head. She said she hadn't, but when he pressed her she said she may have years before. With the voices at a crescendo, Rhys knew this was the right moment. He took a gold ring off one finger and laid it aside—it had been a gift from his father and he didn't want to kill Bianca while wearing it. Then he struck Bianca in the face and put his arm around her throat. He tightened his grip. Bianca struggled, but he told her she would not live through this.

In our interview, I asked Rhys whether Bianca had said anything to him during the attack. He paused for a long moment, looking distracted and distressed, before finally answering, though only at the behest of the voice in his head. He told me that Bianca had said, 'I want to say goodbye to my son', and that he'd replied, 'No, he'll know', before tightening his grip for about ten minutes until she stopped moving.

When Rhys finally got out of the van, he felt confused. He thought he should be feeling good because he'd finally achieved the killing, but he suddenly felt he'd done something terrible. The voice was congratulating him, but Rhys couldn't feel any satisfaction. He also realised that no-one would understand why he'd had to do it. How could he possibly explain the god-voice, or the telepathic conversations with Bianca to plan her death? He knew he had to cover the whole thing up, though he'd made no plan for that contingency. He quickly settled on a random attack by two assailants, smashing his phone and bashing his face hard against the van to produce the necessary injury. Then he drove down to his house, sounding the horn in the driveway to get his family to come out. By the time he'd blurted out his story, he was in tears, 'all over the place'. Looking down at Bianca's lifeless body, he realised he loved her.

Rhys was almost able to convince himself that his account to police was true. When, two days after the crime, Bianca's mother accused him of murdering her daughter, he became quite defensive with her. Already he had firmly adopted the role of grieving victim. It wasn't too difficult, because the grief was real.

After the murder, Rhys continued to experience telepathic communication, now with Bianca's spirit—he believed she was somewhat understanding of what he'd done but also angry and sad. The police record of interview hinted at this underlying psychosis. Rhys talked about 'genres and styles and things' and about categorising everything, themes from his telepathic conversation with Bianca. Apart from that, however, he let nothing slip, and it's doubtful the police recognised the significance of such vague and obtuse statements.

This case was one of the most difficult ever to come before the Mental Health Court. The fact that Rhys had manufactured a story and stuck to it for many months after being charged, at the same time presenting himself as a grieving victim, gave rise to understandable scepticism on the part of the prosecution. Later indications of a serious psychotic illness leading to the murder were seen as another false story produced by a proven malingerer. The fact that he'd given accounts to the treating psychiatrists early on that differed from his later story to assessing psychiatrists also complicated the process.

The psychiatric evidence eventually aligned to the opinion that Rhys was a seriously ill young man who had a range of very significant symptoms consistent with a diagnosis of chronic, treatment-resistant schizophrenia called paranoid type. At the time of the murder, his psychotic illness deprived him of the capacity to know that he was doing wrong in a moral sense. This opinion held, despite Rhys's cover-up. This has been referred to as 'double bookkeeping', where a psychotic person is capable of knowing others will see his behaviour as illegal, while he is himself convinced of the rightness and necessity of his behaviour because of the power of his delusional beliefs. In Rhys's case, the psychosis drove him to behave in a murderous manner that would otherwise have been completely out of character.

I found giving evidence in this case quite frustrating. I was in no doubt as to Rhys's diagnosis and dangerousness, but initially the prosecutor was not ready to listen, especially when I tried to point to evidence of violent fantasies and command hallucinations going back years before the murder. It was only when further concerns came from the new treating psychiatrist at the secure hospital that the court saw the necessity to clarify the evidence and get a further report, which confirmed my opinion. When it became clear to staff at the hospital that Rhys was still having thoughts about and impulses to assault personnel, he was treated with strict security measures in place—no staff members were to interview him alone.

I felt vindicated. My years of experience had taught me not to expect that courts would always agree with me, and not to take it personally when they did not. But in this case, I was greatly concerned that Rhys might be returned to jail after inadequate treatment, with a high risk that someone else in the prison might become another victim. At least in hospital, further treatments would have a chance of success, and in the meantime the risk would be known and managed.

This case was unusually combative for the Mental Health Court, which generally takes a more inquisitorial approach, similar to the French legal approach. It was the strong suggestion early on that Rhys was malingering, which for some time was even entertained by his treating psychiatrist, that caused the prosecution to be so determined to pursue that line, even if it meant ignoring the evidence pointing to psychosis as the real motivator. Fortunately, the real state of affairs eventually emerged and Rhys's dangerousness was fully recognised. If this had not been the case, yet another dire warning might have been ignored, and Rhys might have gone on to murder again.

The court went on to make a finding of unsoundness of mind, and applied a forensic order requiring Rhys's continued detention for treatment as a patient at the secure hospital, with no leave. Strong comment was made that if in the future any leave or discharge was to be considered, it should be done with great care and consideration of Rhys's potential to be very secretive about his symptoms. Despite the detailed judgment—it covered forty-seven pages—the prosecution was still not convinced, and an appeal went to the Court of Appeal. However, this was not allowed, and Rhys remained in the hospital.

Bianca's mother made a victim impact statement in the court and also spoke to *The Courier Mail*, pleading that Rhys never be released or given leave from the hospital:

He was a charming boy next door who was fascinated by murder and fooled many. My sweet darling daughter's last minutes were like a horror movie—full of betrayal, evil and pain—though unfortunately real. It would be truly dangerous for anyone to make a decision that he is improving.

Bianca is the primary victim, with her family a close second. But it should not be forgotten that Rhys and his family are also victims—of Rhys's illness, which has wrought a dreadful toll on him and them. The ripple effects of a murder run wide.

Rhys is an example of a psychotic murderer. This refers to a person suffering from a severe mental illness that produces a disordered state of mind, which renders them out of touch with reality. They live in a world not governed by normal rules and laws but, rather, dictated by delusions or hallucinations, and have a grossly distorted perception of what is occurring around them. Most psychoses do not result in murder, or even in lesser degrees of violence. But some do, arising in a person with no history of violent behaviour and for whom violence is quite out of character.

The clinical conditions that might produce violence, and potentially murder, include psychotic depression, delusional disorder, schizophrenia, and drug-induced psychosis. Relevant symptoms may be depressive delusions of despair, such as in severe post-natal depression; delusions of persecution; hearing voices instructing the person to attack (command hallucinations); or quite bizarre ideas such as believing that a relative's body has been taken over by some evil entity (Capgras syndrome). There is really no limit to the capacity of the human brain for extraordinary experiences when a psychotic process deranges its biochemistry.

Forensic psychiatrists have a crucial role to play in the assessment and treatment of psychotic murderers. Psychiatrists in clinical practice address the issue of risk of violence regarding severely ill patients on a daily basis, in order to prevent murder. We will never know how many times we have succeeded in doing that. We do know only too clearly when our efforts have not been effective in preventing a serious violent event. Every such failure is followed by great concern and regret, with much soul-searching by the clinician, who uses the retrospectoscope to see if somehow the violent turn of events could have been foreseen and prevented. But prediction is a perilously difficult process, and all of us will fail at some stage to prevent an awful outcome, whether it's a suicide, murder or combination of both. It is something we have to strive to get better at, while knowing we will never be perfect.

Rhys's killer instinct was released by the severe psychosis he suffered from. He lived in a false world where the moral and behavioural lessons with which he had been raised no longer held sway. His delusional beliefs and command hallucinations became his new reality, and he acted on the basis that those strange ideas and experiences were true. His rational mind was corrupted beyond his control by the schizophrenic changes in his brain.

THE DISEASED BRAIN: GUILTY OR NOT?

The functioning of the mind is intimately connected to the proper functioning of the brain, and there are myriad structural and bio-chemical issues that can go wrong. Some of the potential negative influences are obvious—a head injury, a blockage in the arteries in the brain, or infection such as encephalitis. Other diseases are the result of much more subtle dysfunction. Depression, bipolar affective disorder and schizophrenia are all brought about through disordered biochemistry in the brain, sometimes with structural abnormali-ties contributing. Here, the balance between the brain's chemical neurotransmitters—a deficiency or excess of one or another—is rel-evant. For example, serotonin deficiency is important in depression, dopamine excess in schizophrenia. But exactly how these imbalances bring about such major illnesses, and the underlying causes, remains fairly obscure.

When the balance of brain biochemistry goes awry, the effects on the mind can be dramatic. Symptoms may range across a spectrum, including mood changes such as depression or mania, hearing voices or seeing visions that do not arise from real outside events, disordered thinking, paranoia and delusional beliefs. Any condition in which the sufferer loses contact with reality and inhabits a delusional inner world, peopled by hallucinated experiences, is called a psychosis. The sufferer will often lose all insight and may then behave as if their psychotic experiences are reality.

In such a state, a crime may be committed, and that then raises questions about the person's legal capacities. Should a mentally ill person acting in response to delusional beliefs or hallucinations, and out of touch with reality, be held accountable in the same way as a person with a healthy mind? How these matters have been dealt with has varied greatly depending upon the period in history when the offence occurred, and from country to country, even in modern times. Even within one country there will be some variance between different legal jurisdictions.

The modern application of the law regarding a mental illness defence against a charge has its origins in English-speaking legal traditions and in the legacy of a man called Daniel M'Naghten (pronounced and often spelt as 'McNaughten' these days), who was acquitted of murder in 1843 in London. Daniel M'Naghten had developed a paranoid psychosis, with delusions involving then British prime minister Sir Robert Peel. His delusional thinking drove him to believe the PM was going to kill him, so he decided to get Peel first. He went to Whitehall and, having spied Peel walking down the street, fired his gun at him. In fact, it was a case of mistaken identity. M'Naghten had actually shot the PM's private secretary, Edward Drummond, who died five days later. M'Naghten was charged with murder. Subsequent events led to the definition of legal insanity that would shape criminal codes throughout the English-speaking world.

According to the prevailing practice, medical experts examined M'Naghten and declared him to be psychotic. He was found not guilty by reason of insanity. Such a high-profile case achieved enormous publicity, and there was widespread dissent about how such a decision had been made. The House of Lords responded to the outcry by ordering the Lords of Justice of the Queen's Bench to define criminal insanity more precisely. They declared that insanity could become a defence to criminal charges if:

> At the time of the committing of the act, the party accused was labouring under such a defect of reason, from a disease of the mind, as not to know the nature and quality of the act he was doing; or, if he did know it, that he did not know he was doing what was wrong. [*Queen v. M'Naghten*, 8 Eng. Rep. 718(1843)]

This landmark case moved the legal system on from the more impressionistic judgments of the past, when final declarations of insanity had rested with the monarch at the time. The two basic issues under the M'Naghten rules, in plain English, were:

1. Did the offender know *what* they were doing, such as shooting a gun; and if so
2. Did they know it was *wrong*?

Lawyers and judges love words and can argue all day about what they really mean. They have had a field day interpreting and, through case law, modifying the M'Naghten rules for different jurisdictions around the world.

Argument has swirled around whether knowing wrong means knowledge of legal wrongfulness or moral wrongfulness. A person may commit an act knowing it is against the law, but may be so deluded that those beliefs lead them to the decision that their illegal act is morally the only path to take. They may believe, for instance, that a devil has taken over the body of their mother and may hear the voice of God telling them to kill her in order to save the world. After killing her, the person might then contact the police to report what they have done. Their lack of knowledge of moral wrongfulness, while appearing to know that the act might be seen as illegal by the police, will likely be seen as satisfying the M'Naghten definition of not knowing they were doing wrong.

Many jurisdictions have seen it as necessary to expand the two capacities in the M'Naghten rules to three, adding the capacity to control one's actions, the so-called volitional capacity. This is important in cases such as the severe manic phase of bipolar disorder, where huge increases in energy and drive and uninhibited psychotic grandiose impulses overwhelm the normal controls over behaviour. It is important to remember that these definitions of capacities relevant to an insanity defence can only apply if there is a disease of the mind underlying the behaviour. Normal passion, anger or despair unrelated to a diagnosable mental disease is not covered. Murder is still murder if there is no disease present sufficient to deprive the person of the capacities.

The role of drugs and alcohol causing intoxication and complicating mental illness has also bedevilled the decision-making in many cases before the courts. Is the illness alone producing the deprivation of capacity, or is it the combination of that illness with intoxication that is necessary? That dilemma has produced variations in case law in different jurisdictions in recent decades, partly in response to cases such as that of a man called Bromage.

Bromage was employed by the Queensland Government to store toxic pesticides. He became contaminated by the poisons and developed a deep psychotic depression. One Saturday night, when drinking very heavily with a friend, he became paranoid and delusional and cut his mate's throat. He received a defence of unsoundness of mind (insanity), the result of a combination of a mental disease (the organic depressive illness) and severe alcoholic intoxication. By the time he came to trial, the poison had cleared from his system, the depressive illness had resolved, and he was immediately released into the community.

This case caused consternation because Bromage's voluntary heavy alcohol use was such a major part of the offence, and this seemed to be an unfair or unjust means of achieving a psychiatric defence. The law was subsequently changed to exclude voluntary intoxication with alcohol or drugs as a contributor to any extent to a mental state producing deprivation of relevant mental capacities. However, involuntary intoxication, such as having your drink spiked, could still be relevant to a defence.

While this was seen as a necessary change to the law, the precedent has produced many cases of complex argument and difficult decision-making for the courts. There can be disagreement about what constitutes intoxication. Drugs such as marijuana can stay in the system for a long time. When does that cease to be intoxication? Drugs such as amphetamines can cause psychotic symptoms while present in the body, but when used for some time they may also cause a drug-induced psychosis, which can persist for well after the use of drugs has ceased. So the borderline between intoxication and secondary psychosis (the latter possibly qualifying for a defence) becomes a grey area. As a psychiatrist trying to give clear advice to the courts, I can say that the issue of intoxication can be very difficult. Clinical opinions and legal judgments are not always a good match.

5

DEATH AT BIRTH

The ambulance switched off its siren as it turned into the grounds of the Royal Brisbane and Womens' Hospital and moved into the parking bay outside the emergency department. There was a quick handover by the paramedics of their patient, 36-year-old Sursaree Chand, to the triage staff. She had lost a lot of blood and her blood pressure had been low when she was first attended to at her home in Brisbane's outer suburbs. Intravenous fluids had helped, but she still required urgent medical attention.

It was mid-afternoon on Australia Day 2012 when the first of three triple-zero calls was received from the Chand home. The male caller hung up without speaking when the first two calls were taken, about six minutes apart. The ambulance service was notified by the triple-zero service and they called the mobile number used to make the calls. Ronal Chand, Sursaree's 36-year-old husband, told them there was no longer an emergency and that he'd only wanted some medical advice. Then, only eight minutes later, he had phoned triple zero again and asked for an ambulance because his wife was bleeding profusely.

The paramedics found that Sursaree had vaginal bleeding and she was in shock. They asked whether Sursaree could have been pregnant. Ronal said this was not the case, that it was the first day of her period; Sursaree also denied being pregnant. However, after closer examination, paramedics discovered a severed umbilical cord protruding from Sursaree's vagina. Even then she denied a pregnancy, saying that she'd had a negative pregnancy test three weeks earlier.

Later, at the hospital, an ultrasound of the uterus showed a placenta, which was delivered by controlled cord traction. There was no sign of a baby. Sursaree continued to deny having been pregnant or delivering a child. Police were then notified because of the obvious concern that a child had been born and it was not with its mother. Serious concerns were held for the baby's welfare.

Police spoke to Ronal, whose story had changed. He admitted his wife had been pregnant but said she had had a miscarriage. A search of the Chand residence was carried out. As a police constable investigated the garage, he noticed a laundry area, with a washer and dryer. He opened the washing machine and found it was full of sheets and towels, all quite hot, which meant the machine had recently been operating. Putting a hand into the machine, the constable was horrified to feel a baby's body wrapped up in one of the sheets. It appeared to have been cleaned of much of its vernix, the substance that normally coats a newborn child. The remains of a severed cord were attached to the umbilicus.

The infant's body was taken to a forensic centre for a post-mortem examination. She was a full-term female child weighing 3590 grams. She had been a viable birth, having taken at least a few breaths of air. The cause of death was unclear, but the pathologist surmised it could have been from hyperthermia (elevated body temperature), hypothermia (low body temperature) or asphyxia.

According to the statements given to police, Sursaree and Ronal had married in 1997, when they were both twenty-one years old. They had been raised in Fijian Hindu families, knowing each other as neighbours throughout their childhoods and then marrying by arrangement between their two families. They had four daughters, ranging in age from two to eight years. Sursaree told police that, on the day of the infant's death, she had taken a nap at home with her two-year-old. She awoke to find her husband and other three daughters had left the house—entering the garage, she saw that their car was gone and guessed that Ronal had taken the older girls to a nearby park. As she turned to go back into the house, she felt a sudden gush of blood between her legs. She fell to the floor, desperate to get to the phone in the kitchen to call Ronal but unable to do so. At that point the garage door began to open, and Sursaree waved to Ronal to stop the car in the driveway. He wanted to call an ambulance but she told him not to. He helped her wash off the blood, but the bleeding continued and Ronal had no choice but to call for help. Sursaree again denied having been pregnant and could not recall anything else that had occurred. Ronal gave a similar story, although it contradicted what he'd said earlier about Sursaree being pregnant and miscarrying.

Interviews with family, friends and neighbours were much more revealing. Many had noticed Sursaree putting on a great deal of weight over the previous six months and that she'd been a lot slower moving around than normal, and had been sure she was pregnant. One female neighbour described her as 'the Indian lady who is heavily pregnant and looks as if she is about to drop the baby any day now'. Sursaree and Ronal were repeatedly asked about a pregnancy, but the couple denied it. Some relatives phoned Sursaree's mother in Fiji because they were concerned she was lying. When Sursaree's mother called to talk to her, she denied a pregnancy and was rude and abrupt. Police also obtained a family video taken at the eight-year-old daughter's birthday party three months earlier. In that video, Sursaree was obviously pregnant.

Disturbingly, one of Ronal's sisters, who had helped care for the Chand's four daughters right after Sursaree was taken to hospital, reported to police that on two occasions the two-year-old said to her, 'Naughty Mummy. She put the baby in the washing machine.'

Witnesses to the recent pregnancy expressed concerns about a similar occurrence in late 2010. Family members had also been convinced back then that Sursaree was pregnant—video taken at a party at that time backed this up—but she'd denied it. When Sursaree experienced strong abdominal pain and started bleeding heavily, Ronal called his mother, saying he didn't know what to do. His sister came to their house and saw blood along the hallway leading to the bathroom—not pure blood, more like the mucus-like blood that occurs at the beginning of labour. Sursaree would only open the bathroom door a little and told her sister-in-law that she was having a heavy period. Ronal then drove his wife to hospital, where she reported heavy vaginal bleeding but no pregnancy. Blood tests and an ultrasound confirmed Sursaree had recently been pregnant, but no foetal matter was detected. The hospital doctor was satisfied that Sursaree had miscarried, seemingly unaware of what appeared to have been an advanced stage of pregnancy.

Sursaree consistently denied any pregnancy in 2010, except on one occasion in August 2012 when interviewed by a treating psychiatrist. For some reason she gave an open account of what had happened, only to then resume claiming not to recall any such thing. She told the psychiatrist that in 2010 she had indeed become pregnant, but she didn't tell anyone because she was frightened of what would happen to her. She said she'd given birth to a tiny female but the baby wasn't breathing, and she'd become scared. She put the baby in a plastic bag and threw it away—the body was never discovered. She said she'd continued to have periods throughout that pregnancy and was confused, but she thought she might have been seven months pregnant when she gave birth.

The police also discovered that all had not been rosy between Sursaree and Ronal over the years. It appeared that Ronal had had at least one affair, beginning in 2010, though it may have involved multiple liaisons. Sursaree had known about the affair and made abusive phone calls to the woman involved, sometimes using a pseudonym. There was other evidence of relationship problems. Ronal liked to use marijuana and he had become violent with Sursaree, causing bruising in at least one episode. He told one friend that he was angry with his wife because she had 'aborted his two twin boys', and he was also reported to have said that he didn't want another child unless it was a boy. He had even told some people that he and his wife were separated. In fact, Centrelink records revealed that the couple had declared they were separated but living under the same roof, and received benefits accordingly.

Some family members thought that, for a few months before her baby's death in 2012, Sursaree had been more distant, rather irritable, and not looking after her house in her usual neat fashion. This could have been an indirect sign that all was not well with her, but there was no more significant indication of mental illness before the events of that Australia Day. Sursaree had no known history of any criminal offences.

Following Sursaree's admission to hospital, the consultation-liaison psychiatrist assessed her as having anxiety and depression. She continued to deny having been pregnant or having any memory of giving birth to a baby, seemingly having no insight into her situation. The psychiatrist was sufficiently concerned to have Sursaree transferred to the Prince Charles Hospital psychiatric unit, under the *Mental Health Act*, for further assessment and treatment. There, a diagnosis of a major depressive episode was made and her antidepressant dosage was increased. She was discharged two weeks later.

The day after she returned home, Sursaree was contacted by a social worker from the Department of Child Safety, who told her she was not allowed to live under the same roof as her four daughters. In view of the allegation of murder, there was concern for the safety of her children, while the diagnosis of a depressive illness was also a major factor. Sursaree was devastated by the decision and expressed the possibility of self-harm, whereupon she was immediately readmitted to the psychiatric unit. This time she was there for a month, experiencing fluctuating levels of suicidality.

Sursaree was discharged to community treatment follow-up—
her daughters had been sent to stay with Ronal's parents—but the
next day, while attending a review interview, she collapsed in distress.
Yet again she returned to the inpatient unit, where her medication
was increased, with the addition of an antipsychotic. It was during
this admission that Sursaree reported for the first time that she'd
started hearing voices at night. They sounded like her own and those
of her in-laws, speaking in Hindi.

Two months later, while being treated as an outpatient, Sursaree
was arrested and charged with two counts of concealing a pregnancy
and two counts of murder. She was incarcerated at the city watchhouse and later transferred to the Brisbane Women's Correctional
Centre. At the watchhouse, Sursaree had been assessed by the forensic psychiatry service. She'd reported ongoing depressive symptoms,
suicidal ideation and prominent auditory and visual hallucinations, and had begun taking a new antipsychotic. In the prison, a
psychiatrist from the facility's mental health service took over her
treatment. She was diagnosed with a major depressive episode with
psychotic features, and her medication was again altered. A month
later, Sursaree started banging her head on the wall of her cell. She
said she could hear the sound of a baby crying in the night, which
greatly distressed her. Her condition was clearly deteriorating, so she
was transferred to the High Secure Inpatient Service of The Park
psychiatric hospital.

Sursaree's treatment thereafter was complex and frustrating for
her and those attending to her. She did not respond to a variety of
oral medications in high dose combinations. She remained depressed
and highly distressed, and continued to hear voices, some telling
her to strangle herself, which she attempted to do on one occasion.
She underwent forty-eight individual electro-convulsive therapy
(ECT) treatments, which are used for severe suicidal depression
with psychotic features when all other measures are ineffective,
but each time she quickly relapsed. She only began showing some
improvement when, early in 2013, she was prescribed a special

antipsychotic, clozapine. The following year she was returned to custody for ongoing treatment from the prison mental health service.

I was ordered to see Sursaree in prison in April 2014 for a Mental Health Court report in regard to whether or not she had a mental illness at the time of the deaths of her two babies that would have rendered her unsound of mind or of diminished capacity, and to help establish her fitness for trial.

She was very short and of average build. Her long, dark hair was tied back in a ponytail. Her hands had a fine tremor. Sursaree was housed in a secure area with ten other women, who were generally supportive but teased her about her symptoms. She enjoyed attending the linen workshop, where she did packing and cleaning up, but she was not allowed to use the sewing machines because of past faints and epileptic seizures likely associated with her use of clozapine. She had no record of any breaches in the prison, and had a good relationship with its officers. As yet, no-one had visited her. Ronal had applied to do so but this was still to be approved, as he was facing charges in relation to his role in disposing of a baby's body. Nor were her daughters allowed to visit her. Their contact was limited to letters and to telephone calls in which the children were happy to talk and blew her 'honey kisses'.

Sursaree's background was fairly unremarkable. She was born and raised in a Fijian Indian family that was part of a strict Hindu cultural group in Fiji. She had no history of drug or alcohol abuse and had suffered no medical problems, nor was there any family history of mental illness. Her father ran a service station and her mother was a homemaker, and both cared well for Sursaree and her four siblings. Sursaree completed four years of high school with good results, then stayed home with her mother for four years, as was the custom for Hindu Indian girls. At twenty-one, happy with the arrangement, she was married to Ronal and the couple moved to Australia. Sursaree did some business studies and worked for two years in public service administration, but once she and Ronal started a family, she remained at home to care for her children.

In between the planned pregnancies, Sursaree had two terminations of unplanned pregnancies—difficult decisions, but she and her husband agreed to them. She had not had any spontaneous miscarriages.

Early in the interview, Sursaree reported a very unusual phenomenon. She told me she could see a man standing behind me, holding a knife with blood dripping from the blade, and that this was distracting her. She had had a similar vision during interviews with other psychiatrists and sometimes around the prison. Such a reported phenomenon was, in my experience, very rare and it immediately raised questions in my mind as to exactly what kind of disorder I was dealing with.

Sursaree told me her mood remained depressed and that she intermittently felt suicidal, though at times in the interview she brightened and even laughed about the things she was saying. She still reported voices and ghostly visions telling her to harm herself, and she thought the people in TV programs were saying similar things to her, which 'scared the hell' out of her. But she managed to resist the temptation to act on such instructions by thinking of her children. Sursaree was quite adamant that she had never experienced such significant mental problems before going to the hospital and then the prison.

Sursaree was generally very vague and claimed all kinds of difficulty with her memory. She claimed no memory whatsoever for the offending behaviour. However, this dense amnesia was at odds with her apparent ability to recall such things as incidental daily activities, hospital visits from her children and family members, and the content of conversations she'd had with her children and letters she had written to them. Some simple tests showed she had good orientation but significant difficulties with concentration and the registration of new material, and that her short-term memory was mildly impaired. For someone who had lived in Australia for many years and who had had a reasonable education, she seemed lacking in general knowledge. For example, when asked to name the states of Australia, she said, 'Victoria, Adelaide, Perth and Hobart.'

Her insight and judgement in relation to her current situation also appeared poor, as I discovered when I tried to get more information from Sursaree about the offences. She said she had been charged with 'the murder of a child I don't even remember having, or being pregnant'. She had some awareness of another charge of murder, but couldn't tell me the year of the alleged offence or any of the details. She said, 'I can't tell you anything, I'm sorry. I have no recall. I don't know where these charges have come from. I don't recall being pregnant in 2011. I don't recall giving birth to a child. Why would I conceal a pregnancy? Why would I do such a stupid thing? I wouldn't harm a child. I have four girls with not a scratch on them!' She similarly denied any recall of the 2010 pregnancy.

Sursaree also denied having seen any of the evidence against her. She said as far as she knew she had never met her lawyer, nor gone to court. However, she was aware that she had a court appearance due in a few months. She had no recall of talking to the police or being arrested. She denied placing her baby in a washing machine but recalled a patient at the hospital telling her she had done that. She could not remember a later conversation with her sister when she had asked what sex the baby was and whether it was full term. Regarding her life prior to the 2012 offence, Sursaree claimed she knew nothing about the reports that she and Ronal were living as a separated couple in the same house, and had no knowledge of Ronal having an affair or of ringing her husband's mistress and abusing her. She said, 'Things like that I should remember, but I don't', then she laughed.

The total picture presented by Sursaree was a complex and puzzling one. The murder and disposal of a newborn child is a uniquely disturbing crime. The killing of two in succession is especially rare. As a psychiatrist, when I hear of the killing of an infant, my thoughts immediately turn to probable psychosis. The puerperal period, surrounding the birth of a child, is a time of particular stress and change for the family, but especially the mother. She has weathered the pregnancy, with its physical and emotional issues, and has then given birth—even if that goes smoothly, it is still challenging, while if it is complicated, it is likely to be traumatic. She then has the pleasure, and the terror, of caring for a new human being totally reliant on her for sustenance and survival. In addition, there are massive changes in hormones that produce their own emotional side-effects. On about the third day after a birth, many women experience 'the blues', when they find themselves tearful and otherwise emotional for reasons they do not understand.

Most women weather these storms satisfactorily, but it is safe to say that they rely on a great deal of comfort and advice from those nearest and dearest to them, and on the professional support of their midwives, doctors and nurses. If the child is wanted, the mother will be motivated to bond with her baby. That unique bond then becomes the bedrock for the positive development of a healthy child.

Some new mothers, however, are particularly vulnerable. For them, the process can be very rocky; for a small minority, it can be disastrous. This vulnerability may arise from biological factors. The mother may have a genetic predisposition to schizophrenia, depression or bipolar disorder, which might be triggered by the significant stresses and hormonal changes of the puerperal period. In fact, this used to be called 'puerperal psychosis' and was seen as a unique diagnosis. Nowadays, it is accepted that it is only unique in regard to the particular setting in which it occurs.

Postnatal psychosis can come on in the days, weeks or months after a birth. When it does occur, it can represent a very significant risk to the mother and the child. Infanticide, the killing of a baby, can happen in that setting. It will be the result of delusional beliefs and other serious psychotic symptoms in the mother that rob her of the ability to think rationally. If a psychosis were to be responsible for the death of a newborn baby, then it would've had to be present during the pregnancy. In that case, it would have been triggered by factors other than the puerperal period, perhaps starting long before the pregnancy had begun.

If psychosis is not the cause of an infanticide, what other motivations might there be? There might be a complex mix of personality, relationship and social problems. There may be an intellectual handicap. Usually, powerful emotions will be involved, such as great fear and a sense of helplessness, or rage and revengeful feelings towards the father of the baby. The wider setting is likely to involve isolation, rejection, a lack of support, or abuse. Cultural factors may also be prominent, especially in societies where the number of offspring is officially limited, or where a male child holds great precedence over a female.

In light of all these considerations, what can be made of Sursaree's crimes? She denied them when I assessed her, claiming no memory of them. But the evidence was overwhelming, and her denial was inconsistent. The pattern of her reported amnesia was not that seen in a genuine amnesia due to a brain problem, and while the extensive ECT treatments would likely have caused some temporary memory problems, they would not account for large but selective gaps in past memory. The things that Sursaree claimed amnesia about were likely laden with strong negative feelings such as guilt and shame, and she may have pushed them out of her consciousness through the mental process of dissociation. However, one cannot automatically assume the presence of such emotions when assessing murderers. Some people are, for example, incapable of the empathy that is the basis of guilt. In Sursaree's case, her ability to raise four daughters with apparent success suggested she was not an emotionally impoverished person.

The minimal indications of any serious mental illness prior to the offences leaves us to speculate about other, non-psychotic motivations. The 2012 pregnancy was probably not planned, and unwanted. If the child had been a girl, Ronal would not have been interested. He was being unfaithful and the marriage was under severe threat. Sursaree would have felt isolated and unsupported, and would not have wanted anyone to know she was pregnant. It is not known what her intentions were as the birth got closer. If the child had been a boy, would she have accepted it and offered it as a way of healing her relationship with Ronal? Or did the birth of another girl cause such a sense of despair and isolation that she felt there was no alternative but to dispose of the child?

The role played by Ronal in the whole scenario is also not clear. He arrived home when Sursaree was bleeding and had at least commenced labour. She may already have delivered. It is inevitable that he was involved in some way with subsequent events.

The fact that a second infanticide occurred makes it even less likely that psychosis was the motive, since there was no evidence of such an illness during either pregnancy or in the period between the two deaths. Leading up to the 2012 offence, Sursaree was reportedly somewhat withdrawn and less houseproud than usual, but those things are understandable in the context of yet another unwanted and secret pregnancy in an unhappy marriage, perhaps with separation imminent. They could have indicated a mild level of depression, but Sursaree was still caring for her children and attending family events. The total denial of the pregnancy was clearly strange, but that alone does not indicate an illness, especially as it was part of a recurring pattern.

The assessment is made more complicated by the fact that Sursaree apparently developed a serious mental illness after the second killing. Depression and anxiety were noted in the days after she was hospitalised and became steadily more serious as the months went by, to the point that she showed psychotic symptoms and became suicidal. She remained significantly unwell even after her return to custody from hospital. It is possible that that illness had been present in its early stages prior to the 2012 episode, but, if so, it was still mild, with no psychotic features at that stage. In any case, it would seem quite irrelevant to the 2010 episode.

It is relatively common for a person who has committed a murder for reasons that are not related to a mental illness, to then go on and develop such an illness. It is triggered by the stress of the event itself and the person's subsequent realisation of the horrendous consequences of their actions. Arrest and incarceration, along with condemnation by family, friends and the general public, all add to the stress. The illness can range from a complicated grief disorder to an anxiety disorder, post-traumatic stress disorder or depression, and sometimes more severe manifestations. Sursaree's illness was certainly severe, her anxiety and depression deteriorating into a psychotic picture, and she also had complex visual hallucinations and selective amnesia. I thought it was likely that personality traits and cultural influences were significant in shaping her symptoms.

The primary medico-legal questions related to Sursaree's mental state at the actual time of the offences. The subsequent mental illness was only relevant to the questions of fitness for trial and future management. Three psychiatrists provided reports for the Mental Health Court. They agreed that any mental health issues experienced by Sursaree in the periods leading up to the offences were minimal, and as such were not sufficient to deprive her of any of the three capacities relevant to a defence of unsoundness of mind (a finding that would have resulted in her becoming a forensic patient under the *Mental Health Act*). The court accepted those opinions. Similarly, any mild symptoms did not amount to an abnormality of mind sufficient to cause a substantial impairment of those same capacities. The court therefore ruled she did not have a defence of diminished responsibility (which would have reduced the murder charge to one of manslaughter). Accordingly, Sursaree was sent to face trial in the mainstream Supreme Court, which would consider the matter afresh.

In November 2015, Sursaree and Ronal both appeared in court. Sursaree pleaded guilty to one count of manslaughter. The court heard that, in 2012, she had failed to care for her vulnerable newborn child—a child whose body was found in a washing machine. Clearly, the Crown had reduced the charge after considering all the circumstances. The charges relating to the 2010 incident were dropped, probably for lack of any hard evidence. Media reports of the case indicated that the court accepted Sursaree was 'suffering from mental health problems, including anxiety and depression, at the time of the birth and had later been diagnosed with a personality disorder and amnesia'. Sursaree was sentenced to five years imprisonment, suspended after three years, which was the amount of time she had already spent in custody on remand. She was therefore free to go into the community immediately.

The law has a long history of the lenient treatment of women convicted of infanticide, which carries much lighter sentencing options than murder. This is in recognition of the unique context of that offence. Sursaree's case was consistent with those legal precedents.

Ronal pleaded guilty to one charge of being an accessory to manslaughter regarding the 2012 offence. He was sentenced to three years imprisonment, suspended after nine months—the period he had already served on remand—so he also was free to leave the court. According to a report in the *Brisbane Times*, the judge commented to Ronal:

> Your culpability is on the basis that you were aware of the death of your daughter as a result of your wife's failure to take necessary care of her. Given the state of your wife and her blood loss, I consider it is likely that you were responsible for placing the child in the washing machine or that you assisted your wife to do so. It is clear you took positive steps to conceal the birth, including cleaning up and misleading police.

In the wake of the sentencing, the media reported that Sursaree and Ronal were estranged. I am not aware of their circumstances today, including whether Sursaree is once again allowed to live with her children.

The most hard-nosed assessment of Sursaree's case would see it as the cold murder of two infant children for emotional gain or revenge against her husband. Murder most often occurs in the context of strong emotions, but it can be calculated and carried out for either social, financial or emotional advantage. The motive may be obvious, such as inheriting life insurance or property. A man pushes his partner off a cliff while out bushwalking, or overboard from a boat, feigning an accident and cashing in her insurance. A woman slowly poisons her husband so that he appears to have a severe illness that leads to his death, then inherits his estate. If she gets away with it, she might do it to the next husband.

But the motivation might be much more subtle and complex, with the murderer addressing their own deep-seated psychological needs or emotional conflicts. It is sometimes not possible to discern just why a killer did what they did, as they may never reveal their motive. We are then left to speculate on the basis of what can be gleaned from their life histories. Sursaree's crime is more akin to this.

One of the most notorious such cases was that of the British general practitioner Harold Shipman, who, from the 1970s through the 1990s, is thought to have murdered at least 215 of his elderly female patients by giving them a fatal dose of morphine intravenously. It took many years for his colleagues and associates to realise what was happening, despite the warning signs. Evidence of a lot of psychopathology and past misbehaviour was eventually pieced together, but no-one expected these crimes to happen—it just seemed impossible to imagine. Shipman was able to exploit these normal human reactions and continue with his destructive ways, until they could no longer be ignored.

Just as such apparently cool, calculated murders are hard to imagine, the motivations that are discoverable never seem enough to explain why killing was the answer. Is it enough to say that Shipman found his own mother's slow, painful death from lung cancer hard to deal with? Similarly, can a mother really kill a baby to get attention and sympathy for herself, or to take revenge on her husband? In general, there has to be an intense degree of narcissism and sense of entitlement involved. The murderer has to either be blind to the feelings of others or perhaps relish the infliction of harm. This perverse exploitation of power may be expressing deeply repressed anger or resentment. It takes powerful forces such as these to unleash our killer instinct in the absence of severe mental illness.

6

THE DEVOTED SON WHO MURDERED HIS MOTHER

When the nursing home rang, 68-year-old Colin Wilson felt as if his world were crashing down around him. It was 11 a.m. on a Tuesday in early 2008, and Colin had been in his shed making preparations for a garden trellis he was planning to erect. His wife, Jean, was out at her book club, so when he heard the phone ring he went into the kitchen to answer it. It was Cheryl, the nurse in charge of the home where Colin had finally managed to place his mother, Ida, only two weeks earlier, after a long and exhausting search. Sounding quite harassed, Cheryl reported that Ida had become violent towards staff and even other patients. The nurse had previously expressed concern that Ida wasn't settling into her new home, that she was demanding and difficult, but had said they were trying hard to help her accept her new environment. Now she was saying the words that Colin had dreaded hearing: they could no longer cope with Ida. He agreed to go out to the home and talk to Cheryl about the problem.

Colin had felt the weight of the world on his shoulders for a long time before the Fred Leftwich Home had agreed to take Ida, based upon a community nursing assessment that she required low-dependency-level care. The nursing home was one of very few facilities for elderly dementia patients near Mareeba in Queensland's Atherton Tablelands, where Colin and his wife lived. It had been a godsend for Colin when it opened, his burden lifted once he'd believed his mother was in a safe place where she could be properly looked after. Since then, he'd been getting on with his life, doing all the things he'd had to put on hold while he was trying to cope with Ida. Now, the anxiety, fear and uncertainty came flooding back.

It was raining as Colin drove out to the nursing home in his four-wheel-drive. When he arrived, a tense and agitated Cheryl told him that Ida had earlier walked off down the road—they couldn't stop her. Colin said he'd go after her, take her home for the night, then return her the next morning. It would be her ninety-second birthday and the family was planning to come out to the nursing home with a cake to celebrate. But Cheryl was uncompromising and insisted that the placement could not continue. It had only been a trial—they hadn't yet signed anything—and it hadn't worked out.

Colin could only stand there and wonder what on earth he would do next. Once Ida had gone into the home, he and the family had cleaned out the council flat where she'd lived for the last five years, throwing out drawers full of soiled underwear and rubbish and scrubbing the place clean. The council had immediately reallocated the accommodation. There was no going back.

Everyone knew that except Ida. She was too confused to remotely comprehend the situation. Her progressive dementia had inexorably reduced a caring and capable woman to a rambling husk of a person, albeit just as stubborn and determined as she'd ever been. The problem was, her determination was now aimless and self-destructive. Ida's condition had deteriorated to the point where only a professional team of nurses could care for her—there was no way Colin and Jean could accommodate her, nor could anyone else in the family. And now, the only place they'd found, after months of searching, couldn't cope with her either.

Colin soon caught up with Ida. She was tottering along the road at a fair speed, her flimsy cotton dress wet and clinging to her thin frame, grey hair matted, slippers soaked and muddy. Reluctantly, she got into the vehicle. During the early days of the placement, despairing about his mother's intransigence, Colin had said to his wife that he should take Ida out to the bush, to a clearing he knew under some big fig trees, and tell her that if she didn't settle down, that would be where she'd have to live. Colin now thought that if he took her to that spot and made her think she'd have to stay there, in an abandoned car body, she might just come to her senses and agree to go back to the nursing home. He could then try to talk Cheryl into giving her another chance.

Much later, when I saw Colin for an assessment, he told me what happened next. They reached the clearing, a dark place in the rain, dripping wet and cold, and Colin got Ida out of the car. He told her she'd have to stay there if she didn't agree to settle down in the nursing home, but she said nothing. Colin looked in the truck for an umbrella, and when he turned around, he saw that Ida was already trotting off up the track. Colin told me, 'That's when I lost it.' In a split second, he decided that he would kill her, and then himself.

Colin opened his toolbox and removed a wheel spanner, then cut some rope with a pocketknife. Walking towards his mother, his vision narrowed and all he saw was the back of her head, nothing else. He hit Ida on the head as hard as he could and she fell forward onto her face 'like a nine-pin', motionless. Colin put his hands under Ida's shoulders and dragged her off the track. Then her eyes opened and he realised she wasn't dead. Using his pocketknife, he cut her throat, saying as he did so, 'I'm sorry, Mum, I'm sorry, Mum, but my life's finished too.'

Colin told me he hadn't planned to kill his mother until moments before it happened. He said if he'd planned it, he would have shot her with one of the three rifles he kept at home, before killing himself. He looked at me, tears welling in his eyes, and asked, 'Is your mother still alive?' I asked Colin if he missed his mother.

He replied that it was hard to miss her, considering what she'd been like in the last few years of her life. But it was evident he had devoted himself to his mother's care right up until the moment he killed her.

He went on to tell me that he'd cut some lantana branches from bushes along the road and placed them over Ida's body. He thought that would make it obvious to any searchers where the body was. He also took off all his clothes and left them at the scene, so that it would be clear that it was he who'd killed her. Then, carrying his belt, pocketknife and the rope, he went off into the bush, first doing two large circuits 'to put the police off the track'. He walked a long way into the scrub before working out how to kill himself.

Colin was a very experienced bushman and he knew what to look for. Eventually, he found a leaning tree and crawled up the trunk to where it forked. He tied the rope around his neck but realised it wasn't long enough to tie around the tree trunk, so he went and found a stick, tied the rope to it, and, having climbed back up the tree, placed the stick across the fork. He slashed his wrists with the pocketknife, as well as slashing the inside of his elbow, trying to hit the blood vessels there. He also stabbed his groin. Then he said goodbye to everyone he knew and jumped upwards and backwards to hang himself. But after a tremendous jerk, he hit the ground— either the rope or the stick had broken and he had not died.

Colin lay for the next two days where he'd fallen, in a lot of pain, shivering with cold, and unable to move much. From time to time he tried to reopen his cut wrists to make them bleed. He did not eat or drink. When he finally heard the sound of a beating drum, he realised it was being made by State Emergency Service workers who were looking for him. 'Poor buggers,' he thought, and decided to give himself up to save them having to search anymore. When he hauled himself upright he was very giddy, but using a stick for support, he walked slowly until he came to a main road. Exhausted, he was sitting against a tree when an SES vehicle drove up. The men in the car had been looking for Colin ever since his vehicle and Ida's body had been found by a bushwalker.

The police took Colin to the hospital in Mareeba. But there were maggots growing in his wounds and he required surgery for severed tendons, so he was transferred to the Cairns Base Hospital for the necessary procedures, then taken to the Cairns watchhouse. He told the police he didn't want a lawyer present at his interview. He confessed to killing his mother and seemed full of guilt and remorse, explaining that the murder was a spur-of-the-moment decision, with no planning involved, nor influenced by any alcohol or drugs. Colin said it had taken him, by his subsequent calculation, 'exactly twenty-nine-and-a-half seconds to ruin everybody's life'.

In the watchhouse, Colin was closely observed for five days, during which time he seemed to be in reasonable spirits. He ate well, and occupied himself by counting the bricks in the wall of his cell and practising square-dancing moves. He even managed a couple of jokes with the staff. Meanwhile, Colin's family and Mareeba's other residents were stunned by what he'd done. Some understood the pressure he'd been under and that he'd reached the end of his endurance and snapped. They saw Ida's death as a kind of mercy killing. But others said there could be no excuse for what Colin had done, no matter how dire the circumstances. Nevertheless, Colin was a popular, active and very well-respected member of the community, for whom such an offence seemed completely out of character. So when he went to court charged with murder, the magistrate was happy to grant him immediate bail pending psychiatric assessments, because no-one saw him as representing a risk to others.

It was to be two years before I interviewed Colin on order from the Mental Health Court. When I did, I had cause to reflect on an ominous piece of health news. Six months after the death of his mother, Colin had noticed a black mole on his shoulder. Because of his legal processes, he'd put off doing anything about it for another year. When it was finally excised, it proved to be a malignant melanoma, and a more widespread local resection was done. Three months later a lump appeared in one of Colin's armpits, a secondary melanoma growth. Since there were no other evident metastases, he was scheduled to have the lump removed, but once again he postponed the surgery, this time so he could be interviewed by me. On hearing about this, I thought that while his suicide attempt might have failed, fate might now be taking its course. Delaying treatment might have been another way of punishing himself, a reflection of a feeling of worthlessness.

It was my job to get a complete history from Colin, to piece together his background, get an understanding of the type of man he was, and to put myself in his shoes in the lead-up to the murder. I needed to know if there was evidence of a mental illness at the time of the murder, which could have affected his capacity to understand what he was doing, and whether there was any persisting illness, which might affect his ability to understand his legal situation, instruct his lawyer and cope with a trial. To do that, I would also need to speak to his wife, Jean, to get her perspective.

Colin was a thin, wiry man with weathered, sun-damaged skin. He was born and raised in Atherton, where he had an active and happy childhood with his sister and three brothers. He wasn't a keen scholar at school, though he did enjoy history and geography. He was caned occasionally when he couldn't spell properly, but he thought he probably deserved it. He had a couple of fights, but that was the last time in his life he ever fought with anybody. At the end of Grade 7, his teacher said, 'You're fourteen, you're finished, don't bother with high school', so he happily went to work with this father, digging huge barn pits on tobacco farms.

As a young lad, Colin had decided that if he didn't drink, smoke or gamble, he would get on in life, and he stuck to that determination. Certainly, he'd always been strong and fit. At thirteen, he was playing with some detonators when he threw them into a fire, and the resulting explosions blew off parts of four fingers on one hand. But that loss never held him back. At eighteen, Colin was called up for national service. He did three months of fulltime infantry training, followed by three years with the Citizen Military Forces (now the Australian Army Reserve), going on bivouacs, enjoying every minute of his army service. His working life also generally involved hard physical labour. He helped his father build two sets of three shops, mixing the concrete by hand. When his parents' farmhouse burned down, he and one of his younger brothers helped rebuild it. Then they took on the property as share farmers, growing tobacco for six years. It was at that stage that Colin had gone off to see the rest of the country on a three-year working holiday.

When Colin returned from his trip, he met Jean. She'd been widowed after a tragic car accident killed her husband and young son, leaving her to raise her two daughters alone. She and Colin clicked immediately and married within a year, then moved into a house Colin had built before he went on his travels. Colin had previously been engaged to a girl from a nearby farm, whom he'd started dating at age sixteen, but when she qualified as a pharmacist, her father's disapproval of her relationship with the less-educated Colin won out, and the engagement was called off. By the time I interviewed Colin, he and Jean had been together for thirty-nine happy years, with Colin having raised Jean's two daughters as his own, and proud of the six grandchildren they'd produced. The couple had also set up a hut out in the bush eight years beforehand, and they'd spent three months of each year there largely living off the land and shooting wild pigs—they loved that time together.

For many years, Colin had worked with one of his brothers as a bricklayer. When that got a bit too strenuous, he worked in geriatric nursing on and off for ten years. During that time he qualified as a masseur and later set up his own therapeutic massage business, which he ran from his home. It was very successful and he ended up with a very large client base, without any need to advertise. Even when he was on bail for Ida's murder, his clients remained faithful to him. At one stage, he and Jean went on their own three-year working holiday and he never had trouble getting a job, although a few employers refused him because he did not belong to a union.

Colin had a wide range of interests and hobbies. He and Jean had been members of the local rifle club for thirty years, and they were stalwarts of the local archery club. They both loved square dancing, which Colin had practised for four hours every week for more than five years. They also enjoyed canoeing. Colin and his wife were always socialising with one group or another, and he was seen as the life of the party.

Colin's favourite activity, though, was bushwalking. As an activity officer with Mareeba's bushwalking club (he was also a life member), he escorted less-experienced hikers on nine-day walks into the wilderness, giving them an experience to treasure. He loved yarning by the campfire at the end of a long day's walk. Participants on those adventures—Colin reckoned he'd led fifty-five of them—would say that they relied completely on Colin's skills as a bushman and navigator.

All in all, Colin found his life very satisfying, but things began to change over the five years leading up to Ida's death, as the struggle to care for his mother became steadily more stressful.

Previously, Colin's relationship with Ida had always been good, with no history of conflict between them. She was a strict mother, and her five children did as she told them, but she worked hard to care for them: Colin being the third, with an older brother and sister, and younger twin brothers. Ida also worked on the family farm, grading the tobacco. She kept a neat house, made most of the children's clothes herself, and prepared nutritious school lunches for them. She was also very strong and healthy, until struck by the onset of dementia in her early eighties. When Colin had married Jean, Ida was nice to her new daughter-in-law and crocheted things for the family.

Colin's father died at the age of sixty-five, of lung cancer, probably caused by heavy smoking of the product of his farm. However, as a widow, Ida still lived an active life in Mareeba, with a circle of friends and her sons' families to support her. Colin's sister had also been widowed, down in Townsville, and Ida decided to move there to help her daughter with her grandson. Then, when the grandson found a job in Brisbane, both women decided to follow him to help out. Things went well with that arrangement for a while, but before long Ida's health began to fail. She was diagnosed with progressive Alzheimer's dementia.

Increasingly, Ida became picky and demanding. Her criticisms focused on her daughter, who felt less and less able to escape her mother's nagging and negativity over the most trivial things. During a visit to his sister, Colin could see that she was being driven mad by her mother's behaviour; she was nearing breaking point. As Ida had repeatedly said that she wanted to return home, Colin took her back with him to Mareeba for a holiday, to give his sister a break. As it turned out, while Ida was there, a council flat became available, and it was decided that she should move in. Ida would live there until the events that led to her death.

In Mareeba, Colin tried hard to get his mother back into her old circle of friends, and to involve her in activities such as bingo, things that previously she'd enjoyed. But Ida had changed. She refused to participate in anything, wouldn't mix with anybody. She alienated all of her friends through rudeness and criticism over silly things. She became suspicious and paranoid, accusing a close neighbour of making keys for her flat, stealing things from her, and planting nut grass in her lawn. She even harassed the man who mowed her lawn. No-one was exempt from her attacks.

Ida also became unreasonably demanding of Colin's time and attention. She would buy three newspapers every day and demand that Colin read them all to her. She phoned him constantly with real or imagined problems. To try to placate her, Colin would sit with her for a few hours each day, but as soon as he left, Ida would go to another son's place or turn up at Colin's house, arriving at all times of the day, even early in the morning. She became an inveterate walker, trotting all over town. She would stop people and ask them if they'd seen Colin, making up stories about him being injured in an accident. Friends would chastise Colin for letting his mother wander along the roads, where she was in danger of being run over. She nagged Colin to take her with him on his bushwalking excursions and got furious when he said she wasn't capable of such expeditions.

Her self-care began to deteriorate. Early on, Colin and Jean had arranged cafe outings with Ida, but eventually they couldn't take her out in public. She would eat with her hands. She became grubby, claiming to have showered when she clearly had not. She would insist on wearing dirty clothes, angrily rejecting suggestions that she needed to wash them. And all the while, Ida's memory was failing her. She lost things and then accused other people of stealing them. The family put a whiteboard on her fridge to prompt her with messages and information, but the board kept disappearing—Ida would say the wind must have blown it away. She became incapable of managing money and bills, which Colin had to pay to prevent her from defaulting. She wouldn't use banks but instead put her money in a shoebox under her bed. When the family found it, it contained $2500.

Eventually, Ida became unable to find her way around the town that had been so familiar to her. It was evident that she could no longer survive independently, even with the huge amount of support she was receiving. Even Ida seemed to have some glimmer of understanding that a tipping point had been reached, that something had to change. She was heard to admit, 'I think I should go into a nursing home.'

Although Ida had been seen by community nursing agencies from time to time, she'd mostly refused their assistance, and Colin had been determined to help his mother stay independent for as long as possible. But now that he could no longer cope, he asked one such service for help. Three people came to see Ida and asked her a lot of questions, though they didn't ask questions of many of the other family members. Ida managed to present better than she really was, denying many problems, and as a result of either her cunning or a real lack of insight, an assessment was made that Ida needed low-dependency-level nursing home care.

Colin naively thought that the service would locate a suitable placement for Ida and was shocked when told that it was his job to do so. Soon after that, Ida had to be taken to hospital for a transfusion to treat anaemia. Colin unburdened himself to the ambulance driver about having to find a nursing home, and the driver told him to phone every home in a radius of 2000 kilometres, as vacancies were as rare as hens' teeth. It was a task Colin found very stressful and demoralising. It was therefore with great interest that he heard about the opening of the new Fred Leftwich Home not far out of town, and it was with relief that he discovered they had a vacancy for Ida. While waiting for the appropriate documentation to come through, Colin twice took his mother out to the home to show her the nice room that would be hers. On the day of the move, Colin and one of his brothers took Ida there and stayed with her for five hours to help her settle in. However, that first night, a nurse rang Colin to say Ida was playing up and being difficult. They wanted him to go out and settle her. But he resisted, knowing that if he did, it would become a nightly request. In the event, she did settle down and the next day she seemed calmer.

For a brief period, Colin's life returned to a more normal rhythm. He resumed his massage business. He walked with a group of elderly people every morning for two hours and re-engaged with the bushwalking club. For months he had not been eating very well, his sleep had been disturbed, and he'd found it hard to concentrate. Now, he seemed to be getting back to better habits and was feeling more like his old self. He realised how stressed he'd been for many months prior to Ida's placement. The family even made plans to celebrate Ida's upcoming birthday with her. Then the call from Cheryl at the nursing home came through. Ida did not live to see ninety-two.

Jean Wilson gave me her own observations about the events leading up to Ida's murder. She said that when Ida first came back to Mareeba, things weren't too bad. Ida seemed pleased to be there and enjoyed going on walks. For a while, she had some friends. But then she fell out with them all and became increasingly dependent on Colin. Jean thought he was mad to give so much time to his

mother, but Colin was devoted. Her own relationship with Ida
deteriorated, as she found it difficult to spend too much time with
her. She did remember Ida mentioning in her last weeks that she
had lived too long and that she would like to be dead.

Jean said that Colin had become agitated and despondent
during the search for a nursing home. She would find him sitting
with his head in his hands, and his sleep was patchy. But he was a
man who never talked about his feelings, didn't show his emotions,
and never complained. He didn't even reveal his melanoma relapse
to Jean until three months after it was diagnosed. Jean said it was
a huge shock to hear that Colin had killed his mother, as he had
never been violent. Despite how stressed he'd been, she had never
imagined he could do such a thing. She was still finding it hard to
come to terms with it.

When I interviewed Colin, he talked freely to me and was
very cooperative. His account of events was completely consistent
with previous accounts given to police and another assessor. He was
alert, concentrated well, and there was no evidence of any of the
disturbances of thought processes that might be seen in someone
suffering from a severe depression or a psychotic disorder. He had
never had any bizarre symptoms such as hallucinations or delusions,
and had never seen a psychiatrist before the offence. Colin was,
in fact, a man who had always striven to do the right thing by
others—he'd never been charged with any other offences; he had a
completely clean legal slate. He'd been diligent in always carrying
out tasks properly and had dealt with problems in his life through
practical actions. He preferred not to bother others with any issues
he had. He was able to get a lot of enjoyment and satisfaction
from a wide range of community activities, but when it came to
understanding and expressing feelings, he was lacking in insight and
ability. While telling me about the dreadful events that had given
rise to the charge of murder, he showed very little actual emotion,
aside from the one glimpse of sadness when he asked if my mother
was still alive. Jean's account confirmed this picture of Colin as a

meticulous man with strong morals and impeccable past behaviour who did not show or share his feelings, even with his wife of thirty-nine years.

There's a technical term for Colin's problem regarding being aware of and expressing emotions: alexithymia, which is Latin for 'no words for feelings'. It is a not uncommon personality trait, particularly in men, and is not necessarily problematic, albeit it's probably irritating to those who might prefer to be allowed more emotional communication. But in Colin's case, emotions had been bottled up to a dangerous extent and, in the end, his inability to deal with them in any way other than some kind of direct action led to an acute crisis, one in which he suddenly lost the ability to think clearly about anything except for a drastic solution.

There was no evidence that Colin had premeditated the death of his mother until the twenty-nine-and-a-half seconds when he'd 'lost it' and put a sudden plan into action that involved killing himself as well as her. Homicide and suicide both formed part of that one despairing act. His previous thoughts about showing Ida the bush site, or Ida herself saying that she'd lived too long and wished to die, might in retrospect be significant in terms of planning, or the appropriateness of a mercy killing. But I believed Colin when he said he'd never planned any such thing. Perhaps there were some unconscious thoughts that he was not aware of, but in that case we will never know them.

My report to the court outlined my assessment of Colin's personality and the great stress he had laboured under in caring for Ida. There was evidence of some difficulty in coping emotionally in the time leading up to the killing, and of the onset of hopelessness when Ida's placement failed. Colin did not have sufficient symptoms before Ida's death to make a clear diagnosis of severe clinical depression, but he was probably masking a lot of his increasing despair. In the moments before the killing, however, he had undergone a dramatic emotional crisis and could not think clearly about rational solutions to the problem he faced with his mother. He had shown symptoms of depersonalisation, with a narrowing of vision and awareness, this being a defence mechanism used by the mind at a time of severe stress. I made the technical diagnosis of an acute adjustment disorder, on the basis of the other personality and stress issues. I recommended to the court that as a result of that disorder, Colin should be seen as having had a substantial impairment of his capacity to know that he ought not carry out the act against his mother that resulted in her death. If accepted by the court, that would reduce the offence from one of murder to that of manslaughter.

I assessed Colin while he was still on bail, shortly before he was to appear in the Supreme Court for a hearing. On the day of the hearing, he went for his usual 5.30 a.m. walk but did not return. The alarm went out from a distressed Jean and family. A search was mounted, first around Mareeba and its walking tracks, then relocating to the bush area where Colin had initially disappeared after killing his mother. For five days there was no sign of him. Police appealed for assistance, saying that Colin was such an experienced bushman there was no way they would find him if he didn't want to be found. They could only imagine the stress the family was suffering and hoped for closure one way or the other. Then he was spotted by a helicopter crew: wandering, dehydrated and delirious. Guilt, remorse and the pending court appearance had proven too much and Colin had walked off to die, but once again fate had not allowed it.

I had no further involvement in Colin's case. Media reports of the case indicated that he was supported in court by his wife, siblings and friends, who had urged police and prosecutors not to press charges in such a tragic case. His lawyer presented his case as that of a 'devoted son and gentle and caring man of impeccable character' who committed a 'bizarre and peculiar act', which was by nature a 'mercy killing' to end his mother's suffering from an advanced dementia, one that had rendered her grossly confused and aggressive such that she faced eviction from her nursing home.

The court found Colin not guilty of murder, by virtue of diminished responsibility, but guilty of the manslaughter of his mother. The judge took account of all the circumstances, including the fact that Colin was suffering from secondary malignant melanoma, and sentenced him to three years in custody. I do not know whether Colin is still alive today, or whether his cancer has had the final say.

This was a sane murder, to the extent that Colin did not totally lose contact with reality. He did not suffer delusions or hallucinations. But he was motivated by intense despair, with suicidal as well as homicidal intent. There was no doubt a lot of frustrated anger as well, but great sadness and hopelessness were the more important driving forces. Combined, they were enough to turn a previously normal, well-functioning human being into a killer.

7

A DANGEROUS PRISONER

It was late in 1983 when Mark Lawrence decided that the time had come to turn his killing fantasy into reality. The 22-year-old had nurtured the fantasy for seven years, developing the detail, and he knew exactly what he wanted to do—in fact, what he *had* to do. The urge was so strong he could no longer contain it. For years, these particular mental images had provided the rocket fuel for his masturbating, which he did up to seven times a day. Sometimes other thoughts or images entertained him, but most often it was the vision of sexual killing he found most thrilling. Now he had to find his chosen victim and make it real.

Mark left his room in the male admission ward of Wolston Park mental hospital and headed for the canteen, which was accessible to low-security patients who wanted a snack or an alternative to the food in their ward's dining area. The hospital housed some 1200 patients in twenty wards. It was located on a huge site beside the Brisbane River, on the outskirts of the Queensland capital. Down towards the river, near a dam, was a wide swathe of thick bush. Mark had explored the area and knew it well.

The woman who had starred in Mark's fantasy for some weeks now was another low-security patient whom he had picked out during previous visits to the canteen. But he was very disappointed to find she was not in the canteen that morning. At first he was undecided about what to do. Should he postpone the event until she appeared again? No, the urge was too strong, and he had primed himself to do it today. So he settled on another young woman in the canteen that day, Julie, whom he had spoken to on a few occasions. Mark bought a large bottle of soft drink and asked Julie if she'd like to join him for a drink down by the dam. She agreed and they set off on a path towards the river.

As soon as they were out of sight and earshot of the hospital buildings, Mark grabbed Julie by the throat. This was how his fantasy started. First, grab the woman by the throat to subdue her, then rip her clothes off, rape her, and finally cut her throat. The last part was the most thrilling and sexually exhilarating for Mark. It would be the fulfilment of his fantasy. But Mark quickly learned that fantasy and reality didn't necessarily match.

He'd always imagined his victim would be readily overcome. In Julie's case, he believed she wasn't the brightest young woman, and that her chronic mental illness had further dulled her intellectual capacities, making her an easy target. But she turned out to be fit and strong, and not such a ready victim. When Mark tried to throw her to the ground, Julie fought back fiercely. She screamed so loudly that Mark was concerned any waterskiers on the river might hear her. He finally managed to get her onto the ground and put his hand on her mouth, telling her to shut up. She managed to say, 'If you let me go, I won't go to the police', but Mark would have none of it. Desperate to subdue Julie, he hit her on the head with the soft-drink bottle, hard enough to shatter it. He also tightened his grip on her neck. Finally, he picked up a long shard of glass and slashed her throat.

By now, Julie had stopped moving, and Mark realised she was dead. During the struggle he'd wanted to rape her, but her struggles had prevented it. He hadn't even managed to properly remove his trousers, though he'd ejaculated into his underpants with his final attack. He had also wanted to see more blood. The plan had been to use the sharpened pocketknife he had in his trousers, but he hadn't been able to get it out. The broken glass was a poor substitute.

Mark wasn't sure what to do next. In his mental rehearsals of the killing, he'd been able to enjoy the sexual climax without having to worry about cleaning up the crime scene. But now he had a dead body to deal with. All he could think to do was try to burn it. He dragged Julie off the path, put a few bits of undergrowth on her, and used his cigarette lighter to set fire to her clothes. On his way back to the hospital, Mark stopped off at a tool shed belonging to the golf course adjacent to the hospital, where he'd previously done some work. It was a suitably private place for him to clean himself up—he'd suffered some small cuts on his hands from the broken bottle and needed to get rid of the blood. Having done that, he returned to his ward, getting in without any staff seeing him. He took off his shirt, which also had some blood on it, and put it into a laundry bin, then went to the common area and watched television, as he did every day. When Julie didn't return to her ward that afternoon, it was assumed she'd absconded, and paperwork was completed to have her traced and returned to the hospital.

That night, Mark realised his watch was missing. He figured it had come off his wrist in the struggle with his victim, so the next morning he returned to the crime scene. He saw that the fire he'd set hadn't really taken. Lifting up Julie's body, he found his watch underneath her. As he did this, he felt nothing: there was no guilt, no other emotion. On his way back to the ward he threw the watch into a rubbish bin.

The following day, Mark's mind was buzzing with the thought that his fantasy had not been properly fulfilled. Julie had made it all go bad. In any case, she wasn't the victim he'd fantasised about for so long. He was sure that with the right woman, it would all go to plan and his sexual desire would be properly satisfied. He was therefore anxious to find his original target. It turned out, however, that the woman in question had earlier been discharged from the hospital. Mark was intensely disappointed. That night, he masturbated to the memory of what he'd done, but with the details altered to fit in more with his initial fantasy.

The next day, Mark told another patient that he'd found a body down near the dam. He wasn't exactly sure why he did that, but it was probably because he knew that Julie would eventually be discovered, and he figured that prompting that discovery would divert attention from him as a suspect. His revelation had the opposite effect. The other patient reported to staff what Mark had told him and the police quickly became involved. They interviewed Mark three times. In the first interview, he admitted seeing Julie's body, but denied any other knowledge. In the second interview, he was questioned much more closely, but he still insisted he had no idea how Julie had died. The police then took him to the scene for the third interview and he was placed under more pressure to reveal what he knew. Mark broke down and confessed his guilt.

Since Mark was a patient undergoing treatment for a serious personality disorder and problems with emotional control, the police and hospital authorities decided not to place him in custody immediately, but instead transfer him to a high-security hospital adjacent to a nearby prison. There, he would be contained and safe while he was further assessed, and while evidence was properly collected. This included a psychiatric report on Mark that was prepared at the request of Legal Aid, and revealed an upbringing with a great deal of sexual abuse, along with detail of Mark's many admissions to hospital and his severe emotional disturbance. The psychiatrist gave the opinion that, even though he was not psychotic and therefore not completely out of touch with reality, Mark's degree of emotional disturbance and personality disorder was sufficient to have substantially impaired his capacity to understand the illegality of his actions and to control them.

Mark underwent a committal hearing in the Magistrates Court
that went over several days. There was no doubt that he had killed
Julie. The issue was whether, as someone who had, on and off,
spent years in a psychiatric institution, with suicide attempts and
emotional turmoil, he was fully responsible for his actions. In the
end, negotiations between the relevant parties led to the prosecution
reducing the charge from murder to manslaughter. Mark pleaded
guilty in the District Court to the lesser charge and was sentenced
to fifteen years in prison. Nearly three decades later, he would tell
me that he'd pleaded guilty to manslaughter in the belief that he
would be sent back to hospital, but of course he was sent to prison,
where he remained until I saw him for a different kind of assessment.

The Queensland legislature had introduced the *Dangerous
Prisoners (Sexual Offenders) Act (DPSOA)* in 2003, largely in response
to community anxiety about paedophiles reoffending after their
release from custody. However, it was applicable to any offender
who had committed a serious sexual offence. Under the Act, the
attorney-general could make an application regarding such a person
to the Supreme Court, supported by a psychiatric risk assessment
report. If the application was approved at the preliminary hearing,
all the relevant material would be gathered. The Act then required
that there be two further psychiatric risk assessments before the
final hearing, which had to be held before the offender's final
release date. The judge hearing the case would consider all of the
written evidence: reports, outcomes of treatment and rehabilitation
programs, and the cross-examination of expert witnesses.

Having all that information to hand, the judge would decide,
first, whether there was a significant risk of the offender committing
another serious sexual offence after their release and, second,
whether the risk was sufficiently great that the prisoner should
remain in custody for further treatment, care or control. If ongoing
custody was the decision, the prisoner would be detained in prison
indefinitely, subject to regular two-yearly reviews. Alternatively, the
judge could determine that the significant risk could be reduced

and controlled to an acceptable level in the community by the application of a comprehensive supervision order.

A supervision order can contain many conditions, such as the offender not being allowed to access children unsupervised, use alcohol or drugs, or access pornography or social media. They might be required to wear an electronic monitoring device, report on social contacts, obey a curfew, or avoid certain places, such as schools. A supervision order is in place for at least five years, with an option for it to be renewed by the court if necessary. The effect of such an order is to place a kind of external structure around potential offenders, a substitute for internal controls in individuals who lack the capacity to monitor and regulate their own behaviour when it comes to sexual boundaries deemed important in society.

Mark Lawrence was one of the first prisoners to come under the *DPSOA*. He was unique at the time in that the others coming under the Act were serious sex offenders, but none of them had also been killers. The legislation was not without its critics, who argued about civil rights, double jeopardy and ethics, but it was similar to legislation appearing in other Australian states and many countries of similar social structure—ultimately, challenges to the High Court failed to stop the application of the laws. So Mark had to face the fact that he would not be automatically released at the end of his sentence. Rather, there was the very real prospect that he might remain in prison for a very long time if he could not satisfy the court that he was a reformed man who no longer saw sadistic rape and murder as part of his life plan.

I became involved in this case well after Mark had been detained under the *DPSOA*. The court had decided to get a fresh view of the potential effectiveness of a supervision order from a psychiatrist who had not been involved in the earlier hearings, by which time Mark had been in continuous custody for twenty-seven years. That meant that, counting earlier periods in detention and hospital, he had spent most of his adolescence and adult life in institutions and therefore could be described as 'institutionalised', robbed of almost all the skills required to live an independent life in the community.

Not long before Mark's fifteen-year sentence for manslaughter was to have expired, he sexually assaulted another male prisoner and received an additional six-year sentence. At that sentencing hearing he was declared a serious violent offender, meaning that he had to serve at least 80 per cent of his sentence. The judge urged the Parole Board to carefully consider the medical reports before granting parole. Mark did successfully appeal his conviction, after claiming the victim had lied and the sex was consensual. But the second jury also found him guilty, and this time he was sentenced to seven years, with the second judge recommending he not be considered for early parole. The evidence accepted by both juries was that the sexual assault had been motivated by sadistic fantasies and that the victim had been restrained and threatened with death before being brutally raped. It was not surprising, therefore, that Mark had been placed under the *DPSOA* as his sentence was about to expire.

I was ordered by the court to prepare a comprehensive risk assessment. Since I had not met Mark before, I had to start from scratch, reviewing all of the past material and then interviewing him at length. I was keen to gather a detailed sexual and offending history and look closely at his childhood to try to discern the origins of his severely disturbed behaviour.

Mark was an overweight man with medium-length, greasy, grey hair who looked at least his fifty-two years of age. He generally looked unkempt, and there was some evident body odour. There were also quite a few crude tattoos on his arms. He was at first suspicious of me, believing that if I had read the previous reports I might be biased in compiling my own report. I explained that in order to be thorough, it was necessary for me to see all the available material but that, having done that, I would be giving my own opinion. He gradually relaxed and in the end talked readily, albeit at times he was quite guarded.

Mark had had a lot of learning difficulties and went to an opportunity school for intellectually challenged children—he was later assessed as having a borderline intellectual handicap, with an IQ of about 70. He truanted a lot and left school early, illiterate. Over his years in prison, however, he'd taken a lot of literacy classes and achieved a third-year high school certificate. His only job had been with a butter factory on and off for three years.

Mark's many admissions to a mental hospital came about because of recurrent fears he might be a risk to both himself and others. He underwent a lot of tests but there was little to offer in the way of effective treatment. Hospital was simply a safe haven in which to give him a level of care that was not available to him elsewhere. He made no actual suicide attempts until after he was sent to prison for Julie's murder. There, he cut his wrists, and on another occasion was prevented from trying to hang himself with a sheet. He also went on a brief hunger strike after his conviction for rape.

The killing of Julie when Mark was twenty-two was by no means the first official evidence of his sexual offending. Mark was vague and defensive about earlier crimes, but as a teenager he'd committed at least four assaults upon children. At sixteen years of age, he'd enticed a nine-year-old boy into a cubicle at a railway station, intending to sexually assault him, but couldn't go through with it. At nineteen, he followed another young boy into a school toilet, pushed him to the floor and tried to remove his trousers. These and the other incidents did not progress to actual sexual assault, but that was the clear intent. He was eventually placed on three years probation and fined. In fact, following that conviction, he was admitted to a psychiatric hospital where he was already well known, having gone there intermittently since the age of fifteen.

Mark told me that these offences related back to some of his childhood experiences. He said he'd believed his behaviour was normal. He also thought that by offending, he might have been engineering his readmission to hospital to escape the violence and sexual abuse that he was experiencing at home. Regardless, it became evident that Mark's official criminal history was just the tip of the iceberg when it came to reports of sexually aberrant behaviour from early adolescence. There were a number of documented incidents that never progressed to charges but were nevertheless a source of great concern to family, probation officers and therapists.

At age fourteen, while on a school outing, he pushed a girl into a bush and tried to rape her, but then let her go. That action was driven by violent sexual fantasies. He was suspended from the school and his father beat him. When Mark was fifteen, he took a carving knife to a public park. He saw a group of young women playing netball and waited nearby with the intention of killing one of them, but he was spotted, apprehended by police and taken home. Around that time, he also tried to sexually interfere with a neighbour's son, induce a friend's little sister to have intercourse with him, and strangle an eight-year-old girl when she would not get off a train with him (Mark denied the last incident, telling me he'd actually intended to rape an adult woman, but she turned out to be an off-duty police officer!). By that stage, he'd already had sexual interactions with other children at his school, and at the age of ten had been befriended by a married man who'd involved him in mutual masturbation sessions. For some time, he'd also been paying his seven-year-old brother to masturbate him, and did the same to the boy.

When he was seventeen, Mark told his then probation officer that he'd masturbated for years to violent sexual fantasies involving both boys and girls. Indeed, when Mark was eighteen, a social worker was told by his parents that they'd been worried about their son's sexual disinhibition for three years or more. He'd been openly masturbating at home, despite being told to do so privately. There were also concerns that Mark had been sexually inappropriate with one of his sisters. His father even nailed up a door between Mark's room and the sister's, but it was freed, and the sister became pregnant. Mark denied fathering a child with his sister, but he did not deny attempting to smother his youngest sister with a pillow when he was sixteen—he agreed this might have related to sadistic sexual fantasies.

Mark told me that the sexual abuse he himself had suffered began at about the age of seven, after the death of his paternal grand-mother, who had cared for him from infancy—he'd never known his biological mother, and his father wasn't on the scene. When his grandmother died, Mark was sent to a home for unwanted children in New South Wales. There, he was subjected to extensive abuse by both staff and older residents.

Six years later, Mark went to live with his father and stepmother back in Queensland. A friend of his father took an interest in him and started taking him on weekend trips to an island in Moreton Bay, near Brisbane. One weekend, the man threw Mark off a pier into the water, then took him home, made him take off his wet clothes and then 'checked him for ticks'. That behaviour continued for a year, on every trip to the island. Mark told his father what his mate was doing to him, but his father said he did not believe him. However, he then behaved similarly towards Mark himself. He would also lock Mark in a cupboard, and beat him regularly. This violence went on for years, and it was for this reason that Mark felt safer in hospital than at home.

He told me that other men had behaved similarly toward him 'heaps of times', as he grew up, and that over time he 'started to enjoy it'. By the age of fifteen he'd developed a very high sex drive, accompanied by vivid sexual fantasies of raping and killing females.

Since Mark had spent most of his life in hospital or prison, he'd experienced intimate relationships only in those settings, with the exception of the various relationships he'd endured as a child and adolescent. He'd only ever had one short-lived consensual sexual relationship with a woman, a fellow hospital patient. It had ended when staff, concerned about the vulnerability of the mentally unwell woman, transferred her to a separate ward for the remainder of her stay and Mark was forbidden to see her. That was shortly before the killing of Julie. Mark indicated that his distress and anger at the action of hospital staff helped precipitate his crime. All of Mark's other relationships had been in prison, with male inmates, most of whom were considerably younger.

It was difficult for me to get a clear relationship history from Mark. He regarded himself as bisexual and said if he were out of prison he would choose to have a relationship with a woman, but in prison he was happy to have homosexual partners. He told me that for most of his years in prison he'd been involved in one relationship or another. These went on for at least a few months, some for a year, and a recent one had lasted three years. The relationships generally came to an end when the other men were discharged at the end of their sentences or on parole, although the last one had been broken up when prison officers had transferred Mark's partner to another unit, after a vindictive complaint by an inmate whom Mark had accused of stealing from his cell.

My reading of the material available indicated that, in years past, Mark had in fact been involved in predatory and standover behaviour towards some young male prisoners, and that the sex wasn't always consensual. There had been, at least, several complaints from young men that Mark had threatened them and pressured them to have sex. Generally, these complaints had not been proven or had been withdrawn, and no punishment had resulted. However, the later rape conviction was a proven example of sexually aggressive behaviour. Also, many years earlier, Mark had been placed on medication to block his testosterone and reduce his sexual drive. He said he'd requested the medication because he was experiencing sadistic sexual fantasies centred on a young prisoner. But in my experience, a prison would not lightly supply such a drug unless there were ongoing concerns and multiple reports of predatory sexual behaviour. Mark took the medication for some time but it was stopped because of feminising side-effects.

Mark told me he nurtured some hope that he could be involved in a consensual heterosexual relationship in the community in the future. His hopes at that stage revolved around a woman he had met while in custody. She had been on an online dating site and a former prisoner had introduced them. She had corresponded with Mark and then started visiting him, and they had discussed living together and developing an intimate relationship. However, she had since moved to a town 200 kilometres away and her visits had become far less frequent. The pair's plans for the future seemed vague and unlikely to come to fruition for a range of reasons, including the fact that the woman had a limited relationship history. Relationships between lonely women and long-term prisoners are interesting phenomena, generally destined not to survive for very long after the prisoner is released.

When I first saw Mark, he was in the early stages of therapy with a forensic psychologist skilled in the treatment of men with sexual deviations. He'd never been diagnosed with any of the major psychiatric illnesses, but he'd always attracted the labels of severe personality disorder and a sexual paraphilia, namely sexual sadism: a disorder of the sexual drive where pleasure is obtained from the infliction of pain, suffering or humiliation on a victim. These disorders were complicated by his intellectual limitations.

Over the years, Mark had also undergone attempts to treat his sexual offending in group programs developed for people like him. During one high-intensity program, he talked about his sadistic sexual fantasies. At times, the facilitators wondered whether he was a bit too willing to talk about them. These ongoing fantasies were recognised as a major risk factor that could drive future offending, and were seen as more likely to come into play if Mark were feeling down, isolated or angry at the world. Mark seemed able to understand this risk and absorb some lessons about how to recognise situations where his fantasies might be getting stronger, and what strategies he might use to keep them under control while getting the help he needed. But he required ongoing motivation and a lot of supervision and professional help if he were ever to achieve full control, and that effort would need to be sustained in the long term. A paraphilia like sadism doesn't simply disappear.

After so many years in custody, Mark would face formidable challenges in adjusting to life outside if the court saw fit to release him. Before the *DPSOA* came along, he'd nurtured a vague notion of moving to a country area interstate, where he could make a new beginning. He'd imagined he would be on the pension and gradually make new friends, or alternatively, he would set up a live-in relationship with his lady friend. Although Mark realised that he would not simply be free to do what he wanted, he nonetheless had little idea of the ways in which the world had changed since he'd lived out in it. His plans were ill-formed and unrealistic. But in reality, it was hard to see how they could be otherwise for a man with so many limitations and so few survival skills. He had spent his adult life to date mostly being told what to do, in a predictable routine where he was given all his basic needs, and with no need to plan his daily life for himself. He had improved his literacy and education, had work experience, and had undergone a variety of practical courses, but he was still ill-prepared to face the wider world.

This is the dilemma faced by every long-term prisoner. Ideally, the prison system attempts to deal with this by gradually reducing the security classification of the prisoner, moving them from a secure facility to a prison farm, then allowing periods of release-to-work in the community before supervised parole some time before the final release date. In addition, the prisoner is given access to education, training and work experience in prison workshops. All of this is possible if the prisoner is cooperative and demonstrates a positive attitude to rehabilitation. But if they are rebellious, devious, get into fights, use drugs, are sexually predatory or generally difficult, they won't progress beyond the secure prison before being flung out into an unwelcoming community. And if their original sentence is for a violent crime or an offence against children, there will be much more caution and assessment before their security classification is lowered.

There were several major issues that I faced in making a risk assessment for the court regarding Mark. The most critical were the presence of sadism, the strength of his sexual drive and the current power of his violent sadistic fantasies. There were also problems arising from Mark's low intelligence, his lack of insight, and his severe personality problems. But the next most difficult issue was the degree to which Mark could be believed. He didn't have a great record in regard to honesty. Only he really knew what his fantasy life was like and how strong his sadistic urges were. I could draw upon my years of experience in interviewing sex offenders and murderers. I knew what questions to ask. I could home in on particular areas, look for holes in his story, challenge inconsistencies, try to establish trust. But in the end, it was up to Mark to tell the truth.

His probable motivation to present as well as possible in order to get a favourable report had to be considered. He could be expected to regard full openness and disclosure as not being in his best interests. But if he were ever to get the help he needed in controlling his sadism, he would need to allow his therapists and supervisors to be fully aware of what was going on in his mind. This issue of honesty and disclosure would be an ongoing dilemma for Mark if he were released on a supervision order, as is the case with all such sex offenders. They need to share their thoughts and impulses with their therapists in order to get the help they need. But confessing to strong sexual impulses to sexually offend raises the fear of being thrown back into prison because of an unacceptable level of risk. The usual confidentiality afforded in therapy is not available, and it's a very delicate balance for both the offender and the therapist to deal with the need for disclosure versus the risk of trust being breached.

It was always difficult to know whether Mark was being truthful. When I first interviewed him, he told me that his sex drive was now much lower than it had been in the past. He masturbated only about once a week to fantasies of an ex-partner. He also told me that he'd avoided any sexual relations for four or five years. Since the rape conviction, he'd become afraid of being 'framed again'. But when I saw Mark for a further review two years later, it emerged that he'd been in a relationship when I first saw him. He'd concealed it from me, allegedly to protect the other prisoner.

At first, he also claimed that his sexually sadistic fantasies had slowly dropped off and then ceased for a few years. However, when pressed on this issue, he confessed that such fantasies could pop into his head when he saw a relevant stimulus on a television program, such as an attractive woman. He could get thoughts of raping and killing 'for about a minute', and he would then distract himself by turning off the TV and doing something else. He would avoid masturbating to the fantasy because he knew that would 'reinforce it'. He claimed he had been successful in that sense for a few years.

Mark admitted he was worried that his violent fantasies might come back if he didn't stay on top of them. He thought they could if he found himself lonely, isolated, not talking to people, not trusting people, depressed or frustrated. Those statements rang alarm bells for me, because those were exactly the kind of feelings he might quickly develop if he were released into the community without adequate support.

Another vital consideration in this case was the relationship between potential risk and the possible consequences of reoffending. It might be argued that the risk of offending was significantly reduced by the passing of time, Mark's increased age, and the positive effects of treatment. But if he were to reoffend, that would possibly take the form of sadistic rape and murder. The consequences were therefore potentially disastrous—one lapse and a victim could be dead. This left little wriggle room for error when making decisions about Mark's future.

This risk assessment report was a different task from that when assessing a murderer prior to their trial. The issues were not to do with guilt or innocence, nor unsoundness of mind or diminished responsibility, nor fitness for trial. This was all about the future risk of reoffending, and whether or not that risk could be safely managed in the community under a supervision order.

Assessing potential risk is a contentious issue. Some would argue that it's virtually impossible to do beyond the toss of a coin. Others decry the validity of a purely clinical assessment, saying it's too subjective and open to bias. Risk assessment rating instruments have been developed that attempt to apply statistical rigour to prediction, giving rise to numbers and percentages beloved by lawyers and correctional officers, but perhaps they encourage a false sense of certainty. The overall consensus is that, while assessing risk is a very difficult task, the best result is achieved by combining clinical and statistical skills in an overall assessment called structured risk judgement. This was my aim in reporting on Mark.

I first provided a diagnostic assessment. Clearly, Mark was sexually deviant, suffering the paraphilia of sadism. This deviancy can cover a wide range of behaviours, from the relatively harmless bondage and discipline practised by a significant minority of couples, through to the horrendous extremes of torture and murder as the ultimate stimulant for sexual satisfaction. Mark was at the extreme end of the range. It is not really possible to reach such an extreme without also having significant psychopathic personality traits, involving an inability to empathise with others or feel real remorse. Mark scored highly on a checklist for such traits, falling just short of the cut-off point for a definite diagnosis. So it was clear that at the time of his brutal killing of Julie, he had the necessary qualities for a sadistic sexual paraphilia of the most severe type, with no empathy and no remorse. The question was whether that disorder was still present to the extent that he remained dangerous.

The origins of severe sadism generally rest (at least in part) in the early life experiences of the individual, and Mark had seen plenty of early sexual and violent abuse. After his grandmother had died, Mark had had no experience of warmth, love or caring. There was plenty in his background for him to be angry about. Genetics might also have played a part in all of this, and it's relevant here to recall that Mark's father was a sexually abusive and violent man. There is research evidence that indicates inheritance can certainly be a factor in the development of psychopathic personality disorder. There are demonstrable differences in the brain function of psychopaths and a delay in maturation of the brain and the personality that can last into middle life. After that, the worst aspects of aggressive behaviour may settle down. Complicating Mark's sadism and severe personality disorder was his somewhat limited intelligence. Apart from all that, Mark had no other psychiatric disorder or significant physical illness, and in recent years he had functioned quite well in the controlled environment of the prison.

The formal assessment instruments all scored Mark as being at high risk of future sexual offending. The tests were based largely on the principle that the past predicts the future, so from a statistical viewpoint, the stark facts of his past offending and antisocial behaviour really could not have given any other result. The only question was whether the passing of many years, a degree of maturation, some response to treatment, and the slowing of Mark's sexual interest, had significantly reduced this risk. Had Mark taken charge of his past enough to leave it behind him, or would it inevitably predict his future, and the fate of future victims?

My assessment (that of the other assessing psychiatrist concurred) was that Mark was still subject to some violent sadistic fantasies, albeit in an attenuated form, and, crucially, his accounts of these were inconsistent. The problem lay in knowing how honest he was, in whether he could be trusted to be open in his reporting of his fantasies and impulses if released on a supervision order. While the risk might have reduced to a moderate level with age, education and modest treatment response, the potential consequences of any reoffending were horrendous. A transition into the community would be very difficult for him, and the stress was quite likely to produce the kind of emotional collapse that would increase the risk of more sadistic fantasies, and urges to act them out. A comprehensive supervision order might be sufficient to contain the risk if

Mark were totally cooperative and honest with his supervisors, but I had insufficient confidence in his ability to tell the truth when the chips were down. There might therefore be insufficient warning to enable preventive steps to be taken before another rape and murder occurred.

At the hearing, after weighing all the evidence, and after extensive cross-examination of the expert witnesses, the court took a similar view and determined that the risk of reoffending outweighed other considerations. Mark was detained in custody indefinitely, subject to regular review.

That was not the end of this saga, however. I saw Mark again in 2013 for an annual review. By then he had completed a Sexual Offending Maintenance Program and gained a reasonable exit report. He'd also been engaged in individual treatment with an experienced forensic psychologist and was reported to be cooperating in exploring risk factors and preparing a risk-prevention plan. At the court hearing, the same doubts about honesty and risk were aired. I gave my opinion that Mark was possibly getting to the point where a supervision order could be effectively relied upon to manage risk. However, Mark was called upon to give oral evidence for the first time, and his halting and unclear presentation did not inspire confidence that his sadistic fantasies were sufficiently understood and controlled to allow safe release. He remained on indefinite detention.

The next review was in 2015. I saw that Mark had lost some weight, his grooming was better, and he seemed more open and insightful, having continued with his therapy. His age, a degree of maturation of his personality, reduced sexual drive and increased understanding of strategies to control any deviant impulses, all combined for me to indicate in my report that the risk of future offending had reduced to a moderate level. The other assessing psychiatrist gave a similar opinion. The risk could, we both opined, be managed under a strict supervision order, continued therapy, and close parole service support.

The judge was sufficiently impressed with Mark's progress that he decided to release him under supervision. However, that was not to be. The attorney-general immediately asked for a stay, pending appeal, and the three senior judges comprising the Court of Appeal heard the matter. They decided that the reservations expressed in the psychiatric reports in regard to the issue of honesty—whether Mark's reporting of his inner life could be trusted and therefore whether a catastrophe could be prevented—were of sufficient weight that Mark should remain in custody. Mark and his legal counsel took the matter to the High Court, but it found no fault in the earlier judgment.

At the time of writing, Mark remains in prison, and it is entirely unclear if the issues that have to date prevented his release will ever be resolved. The accurate prediction of future dangerous behaviour is fraught with difficulty, especially when the issue is potential murder. The legal system that serves our society in these matters has a difficult task, and it is understandable that in this case it has taken a conservative and cautious path. The price of failure is deemed too high for things to be otherwise.

MANAGING YOUR MARVELLOUS AMYGDALA

How do you control aggression? This involves a balancing act between your reptilian brain and your frontal lobe.

There are certain structures in the brain that manage fear and aggression. Deep in each temporal lobe, which appear at the side and base of the brain's two hemispheres, there is an almond-sized collection of neurons called the amygdala. This is the command centre of our reptilian brain. It performs a wondrous task, every moment of our lives, in helping us to understand the significance of what is happening around us. It tells us whether we should get alarmed and aggressive, or just relax and chill out.

The amygdala is very well connected, keeping in touch with everything that is going on. It does this by being strongly wired to the other important parts of the brain that gather and contain data. The sensory information that comes into the major nearby reception centre, the thalamus, is monitored.

The amygdala also has strong connections with the parts of the brain that store all our memories. The basic structures that allow us to retain memories are the hippocampi (named using the Latin name for the seahorse because of its spiral structure in cross-section) and the mammillary bodies (named as such because they resemble tiny breasts protruding from the underside of the brain), while the longer-term storage of memories occurs in the adjacent temporal folds of the brain—it is incredible that, in a space no bigger than two fingers of tissue on either side of the brain, there is a hard copy of memories of everything that happens in our entire lives, laid down in nerve cell protein. By having access to data about everything that has happened to us, the amygdala can compare past experiences with the new information coming in and make an instant judge-ment as to whether the new stuff is familiar and safe, or potentially a threat. It can therefore be seen as the structure that assesses the social significance of events in our surroundings, and as such it is crucial to our functioning as social beings. Imagine the skill and significance of this little part of our brain, that at every moment of our lives it is carrying out a vital nerve centre function that determines how we deal with our surroundings and experiences.

The amygdala has another side to it. It has a hotline to the brain stem arousal functions that can sound an alarm and set off a fight-or-flight reaction. If you place an electrode into the amygdala of a conscious person and then stimulate it with a small electric current, you will get a different response depending on whether you put it in the inner (medial) side or the outer (lateral) side of the structure—I have seen this done. Medial stimulation will cause the person to be aroused, alert, vigilant and irritable, perhaps even enraged. Lateral stimulation produces a calm sense of relaxation, a not-to-worry feeling. This gives some hint of the power of this little almond and the role it plays in our mental lives.

Back when we were living in primordial swamps, the amygdala might have acted alone in carrying out this task and pretty well always had us acting defensively and aggressively, our primitive killer instinct freely released. But over millennia, humans have evolved a frontal lobe that is huge when compared with the brains of other species. The frontal lobe develops and controls the more sophisticated and civilised aspects of human behaviour and interaction—moral awareness, judgement, mental flexibility, decision-making and sense of humour. It is like a great big wise parent who exercises restraint and educates the amygdala, so that it fires off an alarm only when it is absolutely required. Another ally of the amygdala is a collection of structures around the temporal lobes called the limbic system, which forms the larger control and coordinating centre for our emotions.

The amygdala and the other structures in the temporal lobes are, unfortunately, vulnerable to damage. In a serious head injury, the temporal lobes collide with the petrous temporal bone of the skull and can easily be harmed. The blood supply to the area is fragile, as there is no cross-circulation to fall back on. So in the event of a lack of oxygen, the temporal lobe structures may be more susceptible to damage than other parts of the brain—seizures, near drowning or smoke inhalation are particularly hazardous. Any injury or disease that damages the frontal lobes or disconnects them from the amygdala is also a serious potential problem. Once these vital structures are stricken, the amygdala and the frontal lobe may not be able to function properly. Judgement is affected and inappropriate aggression may result. If extra insults are added, like drug or alcohol intoxication, the underlying damage and dysfunction are exaggerated.

8

A DELUSION OF LOVE

Early in 2011, 36-year-old Toowoomba resident Melissa Englart decided that she had to kill her 33-year-old husband, Scott. Levi Hancock had asked her to do so, and she didn't want to disappoint him. She loved Levi completely and knew she could trust him with her life. He was not physically present at that moment, but he sent thoughts into her mind assuring her that he would deal with the situation. The authorities would regard it as a case of a missing person or a suicide. Thoughts of her future life with Levi and her four children swamped Melissa's imagination. She pictured the pretty farmhouse where they would make their future together. Of course, she still had to work out how to do it. It wasn't as if she had any experience in such matters. But she tossed up a few alternatives and soon decided on a plan.

Two weeks earlier, Melissa had told her husband to leave the family home, and he was now living with his parents. He had not worked for two years because of his bad back and had time on his hands, and he was happy to help look after their kids. So Melissa rang Scott and asked him to come around the next morning, a

Tuesday, to babysit the two youngest children while she took the older two to school and did some shopping. They would also have a chance to talk about the sale of their house.

Scott's relationship with seven-year-old Nathan had always been rocky because of the boy's mild autism, but he got on well with six-year-old Megan and she was missing her father. The two youngest kids, Sean, aged four, and Truman, who was sixteen months old, hadn't really noticed that Scott was no longer living at home, but they would welcome him.

As soon as Scott arrived, Melissa left to drop off Nathan at a special school where he had help with his autism, and then Megan at the state primary school. She then went to Kmart, where she bought a lot of towels, some clothing for herself and some toys for the children; for Levi, she bought a bathrobe, shirts and a watch. Her spree put nearly $1000 on her already stretched credit card. While she was shopping, she received another mental message from Levi, once again asking her to kill Scott, and she agreed.

The next stop was Subway, where Melissa bought two meatball sandwiches before returning home. Earlier that morning she had crushed some of Scott's leftover Tramadol painkilling tablets. Now she put the powder into Scott's sandwich before giving it to him. After taking a couple of mouthfuls, he made a face and said, 'This doesn't taste good. Are you trying to poison me?' Then he laughed, and Melissa laughed too. She tasted one end of the sandwich and agreed it didn't taste good, so she threw it into the kitchen bin.

Melissa had to quickly come up with another plan. She asked Scott to stay a bit longer, suggesting they have a barbecue. She went out to the shops again and bought some meat, a bottle of Coke and some cinnamon rolls. She also went to a hardware shop and bought some kind of yellow liquid with a large 'poison' symbol on the bottle—she wasn't sure what it was, but she thought it would be dangerous to swallow it. In a car park, she poured out half the Coke and replaced it with the poison, but after having a taste, she realised it wouldn't fool Scott. There was no way he would drink it. Before entering the house with her groceries, she threw the Coke bottle into a shed.

Melissa knew she had to hurry up if she were going to take the opportunity to kill Scott before he went home. The two children were in the lounge room watching cartoons. Scott was sitting on a stool at the kitchen bench while Melissa was getting things ready for the barbecue. She passed Scott a carving knife and some sharpening steel and asked him to hone the blade. When he'd finished, she sharpened the knife some more before placing it on the bench. She then suggested Scott sit at the dining table, and when he had, she started massaging his head and shoulders, trying to get him to relax by making him think they might have sex. Scott said, 'Do you want to get onto the bed?'

It was at that moment Melissa picked up the carving knife and sliced Scott's neck from left to right. She had killed sheep in the past and knew what it took to cut a throat. Things now happened very fast. Scott was down on the floor on all fours, making a gasping noise. He'd somehow managed to get his hands on the knife, but after a brief struggle Melissa regained it. Scott didn't seem to be dying quickly enough, so she pulled his head back by his hair and hacked into the side of his neck. She continued to hold his head off the floor to encourage the bleeding, until finally he was dead.

Melissa slowly became aware that four-year-old Sean had come around the corner of the kitchen bench and was standing there, staring, not saying anything. She told him to go back to the lounge room and watch some more TV.

There was blood everywhere, and Melissa wasn't sure what to do next. She went into the bathroom, removed her clothes and put them into a plastic bag, and had a shower, scrubbing the blood from her body. As she put on an old house dress and went to clean up, she suddenly remembered that she'd made an arrangement for a real estate agent to come to the house and evaluate it for sale—he was due in about half an hour. She felt shocked, in a bit of a trance, but she had to get busy. She took Scott's car keys, then grabbed his body by the legs and dragged him out of the house and across the lawn to the carport, where, with a lot of effort, she heaved him into the boot of his car. After washing his blood from the car's rear bumper, she went and fetched some of Scott's clothes from the house and covered up his body, to make sure the kids wouldn't see him. She had grabbed a lot of towels and had just started to clean up the blood on the dining room floor when the doorbell rang.

The real estate agent later told police that when he'd walked up to the house, he'd noticed with alarm that a trail of blood stretched across the back lawn. He was aware that Melissa and Scott had separated again and his first thought was, 'I hope he hasn't killed her.' He felt relieved when Melissa came to the door, although she seemed a bit flushed and unsettled. When Melissa saw him looking at the trail of blood, she explained that she'd injured a sheep with her car and had had to finish it off before dragging it out the back. She'd then asked him if he could return the next day to appraise the house, and he'd agreed. The agent left feeling that the situation was quite odd, but he accepted Melissa's unusual explanation. It was only the next day, when he heard that Scott had been murdered, that he went to the police.

Having seen off the real estate agent, Melissa set about cleaning up the mess. When she was done, she put the blood-soaked towels into some garbage bags and placed them, along with the bag of her own clothes, in the boot of Scott's car. Then she had another shower, put the children into her husband's car, and set out to dump his body.

At this point, she received another mental message from Levi, telling her to drive to the farm where they would live their future life together. It was a lovely acreage in the Great Dividing Range, about 20 kilometres outside of Toowoomba. Two weeks earlier, Melissa had spotted it while out driving alone and had come to believe that Levi lived there. When she had driven up to the farmhouse, an elderly man had appeared and asked her what she wanted. He'd looked at her strangely when she asked if Levi was home. It was then that she'd realised he didn't know who Levi was. She'd decided that Levi was planning to get the farm but had not at that stage involved the old man. To explain her visit, she'd told the man she was out of petrol. He'd driven her to the nearest petrol station, a half-hour away, and then back to her car.

Upon receiving the new instruction from Levi to go back to the farm, Melissa decided the old man was now aware of the plan that Levi had organised, including the killing of Scott; in fact, she thought a lot of people in Toowoomba would now be part of it, helping to cover up the crime. Returning to the farm, she stopped the car halfway up the driveway, told the children to stay inside, and then got out and dumped Scott's body under a lantana bush. From there, she drove to a dump and disposed of the bags containing the bloodied clothes and towels, before setting off to collect Nathan from his school.

Melissa was running a bit late when she got to Megan's primary, and another mother was waiting with her daughter. Melissa was thanking the woman for doing so when Sean suddenly piped up: 'Mummy killed Daddy.' Melissa was stunned, and there was an awkward moment before she laughed and said, 'Oh, kids and their imagination!'

Melissa took her family to McDonald's for dinner before heading home to bathe the children. She was in the middle of doing so when Scott's mother rang, asking where he was. Melissa said she didn't know, that she hadn't seen him since that morning. She put the kids to bed and then tried to rest herself, but her mind was too active for sleep. At midnight the phone went again. This time it was the police, asking where Scott was, as his family were worried about him. Melissa repeated what she'd told his mother, then went out to the carport and scrubbed Scott's car with bleach. She was a little concerned about the police interest, but Levi was sending her a lot of messages reassuring her that she wasn't in trouble, that he would protect her. She remained convinced that, now that she'd done what Levi wanted her to do, nothing would come of it.

At 7 a.m. the following day, the police came to Melissa's house. They noted that Scott's car was there, and when they looked inside they found his wallet. They again asked Melissa if she knew where he was. She said she'd looked everywhere for Scott that morning but had been unable to find him, and had no idea where he could be.

After the police had left, Scott's parents and his sister came to the house. They spent some time looking all over the property, trying to find a clue as to his whereabouts, and ended up in a huddle near the front gate. Melissa then received further instructions from Levi: he told her to tell Scott's family the truth. When Melissa walked up to the gate, the father said, 'You must know something.' Melissa replied, 'I've killed him. OK? Now fuck off!'

While Scott's parents called the police, Melissa put all four children into her car and drove off towards the farm where she'd dumped Scott's body. Levi had spoken to her some more and she'd decided she should show the children their father's body. That would rid them of the demons she'd come to believe were inside their bodies. They would cry and it would stop them getting emotionally hard, keep them sensitive. When they arrived at the lantana bush, she got the kids out of the car and made them stand beside Scott. His skin was grey. The wound on his neck gaped and flies buzzed all around. His eyes were open, fixed and sightless. Melissa said simply, 'Look.' The children just stared at their father's body, silent, except for Nathan, who said, 'Oh no!'

After a minute or two, Melissa walked the children up to the house—the old man was not there that morning. She told them that this was going to be their new home. They played in the garden, jumped on a trampoline, and patted a horse that put its head over the paddock fence. It was then that Levi told Melissa that she had to sacrifice the children, 'Like Abraham and Isaac.' She was confused. She walked the children down to a dam that was behind some trees. She felt unable to harm her kids, so she decided she would leave them there and Levi could decide what to do with them—although somewhere in the back of her mind she had the idea that nothing would happen to them and they would be OK.

Melissa drove home, stopping four times along the way to dry-retch. She arrived to find the police were waiting for her. They urgently wanted to know where the children were. Melissa told the police she'd left them at a dam, but she couldn't give the location, so they put her in a police car and told her to guide them. When they drove up to the farm, they found Nathan wandering around near the driveway, tears streaming down his face. He looked frightened and was reluctant to go to the police at first. But he pointed towards the dam when asked where his siblings were. The three little ones were very hot, tired and extremely distressed. Sean was standing in the water with no clothes on. Megan was standing on the bank of the dam near Truman, who was crying hysterically, dirt all over his face and body. Apparently, none of the children were able to swim. Scott's body was then discovered nearby.

Melissa stayed in the police car while all this was happening. She felt very vague and confused. She told a policewoman about Levi and asked her what she thought about the Bible, then decided to say no more. She thought that Levi wouldn't want her to say anything, and she didn't trust the police.

After interviewing Melissa, police charged her with the murder of her husband, plus three counts of endangering children by exposure—relating to the three youngest kids—and one count of leaving a child under twelve unattended. During the interview, Melissa referred to the children as 'the spawn of Satan'.

I was asked to assess Melissa for the Mental Health Court about seven months after the offence, when she was a patient in the High Secure Inpatient Service of The Park psychiatric hospital in Brisbane. When I arrived, she was sitting in a courtyard wearing a yellow sunhat and reading a book. She was slim, with a freckled face and auburn hair. During the interview, she was friendly and cooperative. Melissa told me that up until two years before Scott's death, she'd worked as an enrolled nurse at the Baillie Henderson psychiatric hospital in Toowoomba. She'd left that job when she was expecting Truman but had since enrolled to do studies to complete a Bachelor of Nursing. She'd had to suspend those studies about a month before the killing because she wasn't able to concentrate and wasn't coping.

When I asked Melissa to tell me what she could remember of the period leading up to Scott's death, she said that she thought things were fairly normal until about six months beforehand. She recalled that she'd started to spend hours surfing the internet, looking at conspiracy sites, and had become paranoid about 'lucifarians' (devil worshippers). She'd also developed some strange ideas about vaccines, which was especially curious given her background as a nurse. She said that she came to believe 'they' were killing people through vaccines in an attempt to depopulate the planet. When I asked who 'they' were, she indicated 'the rich elites who were persecuting Christians'. She regarded those people and their aims as 'the New World Order', and had become convinced they were coming to get her and her children. She'd then started to believe that her computer was bugged, having seen messages on her RSS feeds. She also thought her car and her house were bugged.

Melissa had talked to Scott about these fears, and she thought that although he was initially sceptical, he'd started to believe her a little. However, she didn't share with Scott her belief that she had special powers, including the ability to cast out demons. She thought she was a prophet or something similar. These ideas became incredibly intense in the fortnight before Scott's killing, which is when Melissa started having an auditory hallucination that she identified as 'Levi's voice'.

Levi was an evangelist who worked with the local Pentecostal church with which Melissa and Scott had become affiliated. Some years earlier, the couple had been having marital problems, and Levi had come to their house to counsel them. Melissa came to like Levi very much; she found him to be a warm person and thought he was very good-looking. In fact, when Sean was about six months old, Melissa became quite infatuated with Levi, telling him in a text that she liked him. At that stage they were texting each other regularly and communicating on Facebook, but they hadn't actually seen each other for a couple of years. As Melissa became more paranoid in the months before the murder, she blocked Levi on Facebook, but later she again asked him to friend her on the social network. When he agreed, she sent him a message saying that she loved him, and always had. In response, Levi blocked her on Facebook and there was no further communication, either direct or indirect, until she started hearing his voice in her head.

It was when Melissa had gone to bed one night after a family barbecue and was lying there, trying to sleep but thinking about things, that she first heard Levi's voice. She suddenly heard him say, 'Fuck Jesus, fuck Jesus, there's more to life than kids.' At first she didn't want to listen to the voice because it sounded evil, but when it spoke to her a lot the following day, she became sure it was Levi and decided she could trust him. She started to reply in her head to the things Levi was saying, and from there she developed the strong belief that she had a special relationship with him. He was guiding her, telling her what to do, and she thought she should do as he said.

Levi started urging Melissa to separate from Scott, which she did two weeks before the offence. She told Scott he was no good with the children and she would be better off on her own with them. This was not by any means the first time the couple had separated, but unlike the previous incidents, this time it was Levi's urging that was behind it. Levi also told Melissa she should quit smoking, which she did. Melissa's mind was soon filled with 'a million and one thoughts'. She talked back to Levi in her head, as if he was standing next to her. She was in love with him and realised that he wanted to be with her. However, Melissa made no attempt to contact Levi in reality—she didn't need to, not with all the conversations she was having with him in her mind.

Melissa didn't sleep well at this time; she was very restless. There were at least a couple of nights when she didn't sleep at all, just lay in bed as if in a trance. She was so preoccupied with her thoughts that she would forget to eat. But then Levi would tell her to eat and she did so. Levi seemed to be controlling every aspect of her life. Melissa felt a lot of anxiety, but Levi reassured her that she was doing everything exactly as she should, and exactly as he wanted, and they would have a wonderful future together.

She lost weight and her energy seemed enormous. She was 'going like a bat out of hell, on a high'. She started spending a lot of money using credit cards, building up a lot of debt, which was quite out of character for her. She bought things for the children, for herself and for Levi, all in preparation for their life together. By the time of Scott's murder, she owed $10 000 on her cards.

Melissa continued to hear Levi's voice after she'd been arrested and locked up in the Brisbane watchhouse. He told her that the police, prison officers and other prisoners were all part of the 'New World Order'. She felt that everything was being staged and nothing was real, although she feared she would be killed if she didn't cooperate. When she was sent to hospital, she thought the other patients were also part of the plan and high on drugs, not really ill.

I was able to review the notes that had been made at the watchhouse, and subsequently at the Brisbane Women's Correctional Centre when Melissa was transferred there, and I also had access to her hospital file. I discovered that on her second day in the watchhouse, she was assessed by a nurse clinician from the court liaison service of the forensic mental health service. Melissa lacked concentration and appeared confused—when asked a question, she would repeat it, then pause a long while before answering. Her emotional state was labile, fluctuating wildly from spontaneous laughter to distress and crying. She told the nurse about her sleep disturbance and increased energy, her credit-card spending, and her marital problems, including her husband's addiction to painkillers and cannabis. She said Scott had threatened to take the children from her, once threatening to drive over a cliff with them in the car. Nevertheless, she'd thought he should continue to see the children. But otherwise she was quite guarded in what she said. She didn't mention any of the more bizarre experiences she'd been having, and especially avoided any reference to Levi.

Later that same day, Melissa asked to see a psychologist. When the woman arrived, Melissa greeted her with an incongruous smile and said that she should be certified and taken to a hospital instead of prison. Then she proceeded to sob loudly, saying that she'd killed her children. Despite reassurance to the contrary, she believed this to be true. Then she asked if she'd ever really had any children or if they were 'an illusion', because to her, the family she'd seen in court looked to be only 'shells of people'. Melissa appeared to the psychologist to be confused, with a blank facial expression. She couldn't concentrate and things needed to be repeated for her. Again, she sobbed loudly and uncontrollably, but suddenly stopped, looked up, and said 'a force' had come over her that had enabled her to stop crying.

Melissa was transferred to prison the next day and seen by a psychiatrist. She had a superficial, fatuous emotional presentation, completely out of keeping with her current situation. Her mood appeared elevated and she reported having spent a lot of money for when her 'true love Levi' came to her. Her thoughts were disorganised and often went off at tangents. At times her thought stream came to an abrupt halt, and she was often perplexed when trying to answer questions. She expressed a whole range of religious, spiritual and persecutory delusions. One was that she'd killed Levi, not her husband, and felt Levi's spirit go into her body. She requested a Bible and asked all kinds of strange religious questions. She claimed that Levi had told her to do all kinds of things, finally asking her, 'Will you do it for me … kill him for me?' It was then she'd decided to go home and kill her husband.

The psychiatrist could see that Melissa was out of touch with reality and experiencing a range of psychotic symptoms, including command auditory hallucinations, delusions, thought disorder, and passivity phenomena—the experience of being controlled from outside one's own body and mind. Her incongruous, wildly variable emotional state was also typical of an acute psychotic process. However, Melissa herself had no insight into her own state and for two days refused to take any medication to help control her psychosis and settle her emotions. When she was seen again, she appeared anxious and suspicious, but said, 'I am in here because I killed my husband.' She still didn't want medication because she believed it would open up her mind to demons, but she was eventually persuaded to try it.

Five days later, Melissa described her relationship with Levi: 'He's in my spirit, in my head, where your emotions, will and intellect are seated, in your past and subconscious, with the pathways that are built there where things happened in the past.' She went on to say that 'Levi communicates with me in my head. I hear him, I think, in my head. Is that possible? … I hear him say I need to relax, to trust him, and not to trust him. I've tried to control his voice, well, it sounds like his voice … I initially felt excited and happy when I heard it … I tried to control the voice because I had low self-esteem. I didn't believe he'd want to be part of my life, so I'd go into denial.' She appeared less guarded but still confused, with inappropriate laughter at times. In view of the need for an extensive period of assessment and treatment, Melissa was transferred from prison to The Park psychiatric hospital, and family members were contacted for more information.

Melissa had never before shown any hint of violent behaviour, but her mother had noted some particularly unusual ideas and behaviour in the weeks leading up to Scott's killing. Melissa had got rid of her chickens, claiming they'd been fed too many hormones (which was not true). She also got rid of her dog for unknown reasons, done the same with her favourite horse's saddle and bridle, and talked about having to stockpile baked beans for hard times. Once when Melissa was at the park with her mother, she seemed not to want to pick Truman up off the ground even though he was sitting on an ants' nest. This was highly unusual, as she'd always been devoted to the children.

Both of Melissa's parents believed she had not been her usual self for up to nine months before the murder. She'd become preoccupied with religious ideas and obsessed with the internet, and slowly withdrew from her friends. She talked about home-schooling her children, became very concerned about vaccinations and food tampering, and had some weird idea about Muslims joining the Pope. A few weeks before the killing, Melissa had told one of her sisters that she was repulsed by Scott and did not believe that God expected her to stay with him. One week beforehand, Melissa claimed she'd won a holiday to the United States, and that she planned to take a friend and her two oldest children to Disneyland—there was evidence she'd taken out travel insurance but not of any such prize. The father said that, around that time, his daughter had talked about the 'degeneration of mankind' and said that Levi was the only one she cared for.

Her general practitioner reported that Melissa had seen him for pregnancy-related issues, but he had no knowledge of any past psychiatric history. As far as he was concerned, Melissa's psychotic illness 'came out of the blue'. He had seen more of Scott, a placid man, a 'poor coper', who had chronic back pain and sometimes used painkillers to excess; he'd also been on antidepressants for a few years. However, the GP, along with one sister and Melissa herself, were able to throw light upon a very relevant history of mental illness in Melissa's family.

Her maternal grandmother had suffered from postnatal depression after having twins. She was briefly admitted to a regional psychiatric hospital but recovered quite quickly. Some maternal aunts had also suffered from depression and been on antidepressants. But it was Melissa's mother who'd been most severely affected. At age thirty-six, the same age at which Melissa had become ill, the mother had been diagnosed with either bipolar affective disorder (previously called manic depressive psychosis) or schizo-affective disorder (with features of both bipolar disorder and schizophrenia). She had a number of episodes of illness, manifesting bizarre ideas and disturbed behaviour. Each time, when she became well after treatment, she would stop her medication, believing it was no longer necessary, and then relapse again. This led to multiple separations from her husband. She had about six admissions to hospital, and eventually realised she had to stay on antipsychotic medication to remain stable, which had been the case for the past five years.

Melissa was able to describe what her mother was like when unwell, remembering her staying up all night, burning her feet with hot candle wax, and going around their farm blessing all the posts to protect the family. In one episode, she went in the street naked, praying for people to repent. She shifted her interest from the Roman Catholic Church to the Pentecostal movement and became very interested in demonology. She had religious delusions: Melissa vividly recalled her mother saying to her one night that Melissa would be 'the one that would betray them on the last day'. Melissa was terrified all that night, fearing that her mother was going to kill her.

Once Melissa was well enough, she was able to describe two earlier, milder episodes that were a harbinger of the more terrible illness she was later to develop. At twenty-seven, while attending the Church of Christ, she became paranoid that the church was hiding things from her. She didn't hear any voices at that time, however, and the paranoia settled spontaneously after about two months. The second episode occurred a few years later, when Melissa was separated from Scott and attending a different congregation. This time, she developed the idea that she might be an angel or a prophet. She didn't tell anyone about her possible special status, on the one hand thinking she might not be believed, but on the other that members of the church might already be aware of it. That episode lasted about a month before settling, again without any voices.

Melissa did not have postnatal depression after any of her four pregnancies. But for about eight years, from age twenty-one, she had symptoms of bulimia. She would go on binges, eating huge amounts of food, then make herself vomit by sticking a toothbrush down her throat. She did this sporadically, about once a week, though it did not affect her weight. The actions seemed to be secondary to anxiety and her parents arguing—vomiting made her feel more in control. When she became pregnant with Nathan, she decided she had to stop that behaviour and was able to bring it to an end.

The only treatment of any kind that Melissa had undergone prior to the murder was in her late twenties when she saw a psychologist for some joint counselling with Scott over six months. There were significant problems resulting from Scott abusing prescription painkillers and marijuana and becoming verbally aggressive and throwing things around. He'd also had great difficulty dealing with Nathan's autism, and Melissa did not like the rough manner he had with the children at times. Only once did Scott get physically aggressive towards Melissa, and she responded by 'decking him'— it did not happen again. Melissa had tried marijuana herself once, when she was twenty, but she hadn't liked it. She'd never touched any other illicit drug, nor had any problems with alcohol. She had been a smoker for sixteen years, giving up for brief periods but always returning to the habit.

Melissa's childhood and early adulthood were relatively incident-free. She recalled a good life on a dairy farm, as the second of four siblings, and one of three girls—none of whom would suffer from a mental illness. Initially, she was not close to her father, a hard man who was always off working. Her parents fought verbally and separated in her mid-teens. But later, when her father remarried, Melissa got on quite well with him. Her mother also remarried, to another farmer, but lived in a town a couple of hours drive away. Melissa liked her stepfather, seeing him as having a stabilising influence on her mother.

At primary school, Melissa was a quiet child, but in high school she became more extroverted and sociable. She was good at sport and made a lot of friends, becoming the 'leader of the pack'. She did her Grade 10 certificate, and left school at sixteen after Grade 11 to take up a job on a dairy farm. But after only eight months her father made her give that up and start nursing, a 'proper girl's job'. She trained as an enrolled nurse at the local hospital and enjoyed it, staying on for a few years more after qualifying. After that she went to northern Queensland on a working holiday with a boyfriend, and when she got bored with the boyfriend and the work, she returned to Toowoomba. She spent the next eleven years working at the Baillie Henderson psychiatric hospital. Her colleagues there would later recall her as a somewhat reserved person who was a conscientious and competent nurse, and they had never seen any signs of mental illness and were totally shocked when they heard of her crime.

It was at the hospital that Melissa met Scott, who was a cleaner there. A few months into the relationship she became pregnant, marrying Scott when Nathan was about eight months old. Despite their constant rows, they went on to have three more children, although only Megan was planned—twice, Melissa became pregnant while breast-feeding and not using contraception, meaning the children came in quick succession. Over the whole marriage, Melissa worked whenever she wasn't on maternity leave. Scott, on the other hand, was often off work, allegedly with back pain, which Melissa believed he exaggerated to get a payout from his employer.

Melissa underwent a thorough medical investigation in hospital after her arrest for Scott's murder. The drug tests were all clear, and the full blood and biochemical screens were normal too. The CT brain scan and electroencephalogram showed no evidence of brain abnormality. The diagnosis made was that Melissa was suffering from a schizo-affective psychosis. Her illness had first appeared a few years earlier, with two mild episodes of mood disturbance along with temporary paranoia and some grandiose ideas that had lasted only a few weeks. But it had returned in very severe form when she was thirty-six years old. Her mother had shown an almost identical illness at the same age, and this family history had left Melissa with a genetic vulnerability to developing a similar illness.

As part of an involuntary treatment order under the *Mental Health Act*, Melissa had been given antipsychotic medication when she was taken to prison, and it was then continued in hospital, where an antidepressant was added. Melissa showed a steady response to the medication. Within two weeks of the treatment beginning, Levi's voice stopped talking to her, and her delusional beliefs, including her religious preoccupations, fears of luciferians, and the messages she'd been getting from TV, started to disappear. With this came the realisation of what she'd done. Melissa felt a huge sense of shock and disbelief. Even seven months after her arrest, when I saw her, she still found it hard to believe what had happened. The fading of the psychosis was replaced by depression, sadness, tearfulness, and a feeling that everything was getting on top of her. The addition of an antidepressant prompted a remarkable improvement in her mood, however, until what was left was a more normal sadness about her circumstances and how much she missed her children.

Melissa said to me 'thank goodness' that all of the voices, crazy delusions and religious ideas were now gone. But she told me she would never recover from the shock of what she'd done during the deepest throes of her illness. Her actions had greatly traumatised her own family and Scott's, and left her separated from her children, with great uncertainty as to whether she'd ever be able to have a meaningful relationship with them again. She faced the prospect of years in hospital and a lifetime of treatment under the *Mental Health Act*. Although she was 'craving' a return to work, and to her university studies, her career was ruined, and her reputation in the community forever damaged. In a very true sense, she'd joined the long list of victims of the illness and the crime it had produced.

At the time that I assessed her, Melissa was having weekly visits from members of her family, who took turns making the journey to Brisbane to see her—her mother, stepfather, occasionally her father and his second wife, from whom he was separated. Two sisters visited as well, bringing their children with them. Her brother took his turn too, as did some of Melissa's friends. It was clear that all these people loved and appreciated the woman Melissa had been before and after the tragic episode of illness that had taken her husband's life and shattered her family.

Melissa's children were in the care of Scott's parents and his sister. All the children were seeing a psychologist. Melissa had been allowed to send them, via her family, presents and also messages, in which she told them how much she loved them. She missed her children greatly, and hoped to be able to have direct contact just as soon as that was deemed reasonable, with a view to regaining full custody well down the track.

When she'd written to Scott's parents and sister, apologising for what she'd done, they'd responded by sending her two recent photos of the children. She'd replied with a thank-you letter, but subsequently the Victim Support Service had advised Scott's family not to have any more direct contact at that stage, only indirect contact through Melissa's family. She said she understood that Scott's family would still be grieving his loss and felt they'd been gracious in their responses so far. She was very grateful that they were allowing her children to receive gifts from her.

It was gratifying to see how complete a recovery Melissa had made through the treatment she'd received. Getting control of the symptoms had been relatively straightforward in her case, and she seemed to have minimal evidence of illness by the time I saw her. In other words, her illness was in remission, fully controlled, because of her treatment regimen. But her mother's relapses with a similar illness illustrated the necessity for Melissa to remain on effective medication, probably for life. That necessity and the possibility of future relapses did not yet seem to have fully registered with Melissa. Her wish to have her circumstances return to what they were, albeit without Scott, showed that she was significantly underestimating the hurdles she'd yet have to overcome.

Among these were the likely stigma and discrimination she would face in the community. Many people in her town would be aware of the murder, but they might have remained ignorant of the nature of the illness that motivated it. It would be unlikely that, on her return, she'd be met with universal kindness and understanding. Rehabilitation requires more than symptom resolution. The repair of relationships and community networks is considerably harder than swallowing medication.

Then there was the traumatisation of her children, not only by whatever awareness they had of the actual murder and any memory of seeing their dead father, but also by their abandonment at the dam and subsequent loss of contact with their mother, their primary carer. The extent of the damage would vary with their ages and level of understanding at the time, the effect of the love and support they received from Scott's family, and the degree of assistance they could be given though therapy and community support. But it was likely that irreparable damage had been done to Melissa's relationship with her children. Her determination to get back to a close parenting role was understandable, but it was unclear whether she really recognised the long road ahead.

It was to the Mental Health Court that two other psychiatrists and I reported the results of our assessments. The evidence seemed clear and the opinions were unanimous. Melissa had suffered a severe mental illness, schizophrenia with some manic elements, and as a result she'd been deprived of the capacity to know that she ought not kill her husband. She was deprived of an understanding of the moral wrongfulness of that act, despite some awareness of the fact that it might be seen as illegal—her deluded state led her to believe she would be protected from legal consequences. Her delusions similarly led her to abandon her children, and she was deprived of the same capacity for that aspect of the offending. She was therefore found to have been unsound of mind at the time of the offences.

Melissa was then placed on a forensic order by the court. This is a specific kind of involuntary treatment order used for people who have been found unsound of mind or unfit for trial. Under that order, Melissa ceased to be subject to criminal sanction and became a psychiatric patient under the *Mental Health Act*. As such, she would be detained in the High Secure Inpatient Service with no immediate leave. Her progress to graduated leave and an eventual return to community treatment would be dependent upon the treating psychiatrist's advice and the approval of the Mental Health Review Tribunal, the official body that manages forensic orders. The court did not make any non-contact order in regard to Melissa's children, but stipulated that any future contact with them occur only with the permission of the children's guardian and the treating psychiatrist.

In the psychiatric reports to the court, we considered all aspects of the motivation for the murder. Clearly, there were problems in the marriage: repeated separations, a degree of anger and frustration in Melissa in regard to Scott, his drug abuse, his shortcomings as a father, and his temper. But Melissa had not been violent, except once in response to violence from Scott, and she had been a loving mother and consistent worker to support the family. These real-life issues were not considered to have been remotely sufficient to justify the murder. It was clear that the delusional state caused by the onset of a psychotic illness was one of such unreality as to be the motivating factor in the murder. Without that illness, this murder would never have occurred. It was a classic illustration of the power of a psychotic illness to completely subvert the normal function of the mind and result in behaviour that is out of character and unpredictable. Melissa responded to delusional reality as if it were true. Her normal good judgement was destroyed by her illness.

Was Scott's death preventable? Probably not, even with the greatest foresight. Given her family's history of mental illness, it is possible that Melissa's illness could have been treated sooner, and that could have prevented the final outcome. But that would have required a degree of insight that Melissa had lost very early in the process, and she would not have cooperated. And her previous high level of function would have meant it was hard for those around her to take too seriously the early signs of deterioration.

It is easy to look back with the wisdom of hindsight and say that something should have been done. It is a lot harder to predict a disaster when you are in the midst of the events that come before it.

9

THE ENRAGED MURDERER

Dr John Webber was in his second year as a trainee psychiatrist. He was employed as a registrar at the Princess Alexandra Hospital, which was located in Woolloongabba, an inner suburb of Brisbane, and serviced a large swathe of the city's southern suburbs. On this particular evening in early 1991, he was rostered in the emergency department, seeing all the patients who came in with some kind of psychiatric emergency. It was a role that made him nervous and excited at the same time. He felt the weight of the responsibility of assessing people in crisis and making the right decisions for their care, but he also relished the challenge of making these assessments and testing his fledgling clinical skills.

Of course, he wasn't alone. He had the support of two nurses who manned the three beds in the emergency area reserved for psychiatric patients. They had more experience in psychiatry than he did and were a source of valuable advice. In addition, the on-call psychiatrist was only a phone call away. Most of the on-call consultants were quite happy to be contacted and to discuss proposed actions and treatment plans. Tonight, the person in that role was one of the most helpful senior consultants, and that was reassuring.

At 7 p.m., Leslie Brown was brought into the emergency department by ambulance. Earlier, he had threatened suicide and tried to locate some tablets with which he could overdose. But his wife, Denise, had hidden all his medication because it had only been a week since he'd last overdosed and been sent to hospital for treatment. Leslie and Denise had argued, and she'd called triple zero to have him taken to emergency. Denise did not accompany Leslie to the hospital.

Dr Webber was glad that he had access to detailed hospital records on Leslie's many previous contacts and admissions. It was turning into a busy night in emergency—there were already two other patients lined up behind Leslie whom he would have to assess—and the more time he could save, the better. Nevertheless, he could see that Leslie likely had significant problems and he would have to set aside at least forty-five minutes to interview him. He would need to focus mostly on recent stress in Leslie's life and try to get a clear picture of his current symptoms. He had to look especially closely at the risk that Leslie might currently present to himself through suicidal thoughts or plans, as well as the risk he might pose to others through aggressive behaviour.

Leslie's remote past history and his family and developmental history had been detailed in notes made during a brief inpatient stay at the hospital about a year earlier. Dr Webber quickly read those notes before going to see Leslie in the interview room. He learned that Leslie had been seeing a psychiatrist in a community mental health clinic about once a month for the past year, and had been prescribed an antidepressant to take each night. He was also taking quite large doses, prescribed by his GP, of narcotic painkillers for chronic back pain.

Leslie was forty-two years old and looked as if he'd had a hard life. He was a bit overweight, his complexion was quite florid, and he had untidy medium-length greying hair, reddened eyes, a couple of days beard growth, and several fairly crudely drawn tattoos on both forearms. He wore a stained T-shirt, shorts and sneakers. He was close to tears from the start of the interview, breaking down in sobs at times, but towards the end of the consultation he was more composed and even managed a smile or two. The events that had brought Leslie to the hospital that night were a continuation of the problems that had caused him to overdose only a week earlier.

To begin with, Leslie had chronic back pain that had not been relieved by two bouts of surgery over four years, and he'd become dependent on medication to get him through the day and get some sleep at night. Nonetheless, he was sleep deprived because his pain would wake him repeatedly. He felt miserable and useless at home, unable to be the husband and father he thought he should be, so he spent much of the day on the couch watching mindless TV shows. He was also intolerant of the noise his son and two daughters made in the house. Making matters worse, he and Denise had been having a lot of arguments.

Leslie felt that Denise didn't understand what he was going through. She did have to do everything around the house and had become more or less a sole parent. But still, Leslie felt she had become unnecessarily bitter. Their sex life had also ground to a halt because his libido was non-existent. His back pain made sex very difficult, and he couldn't sustain an erection. In any case, Denise didn't want to come near him, and more often than not she slept in the spare room, complaining about how his snoring and restlessness interfered with her sleep.

Leslie had hardly been out of the house for the past year, except for medical appointments. He had lost contact with most of his friends. Many of those had been former workmates and he hadn't worked for ten years, ever since his back injury. He would occasionally go to the local football club to have a few beers with an acquaintance, and put what little money he had through the poker machines, but he and Denise hadn't been out socially for many months. She sometimes met a few girlfriends for a night out, but she didn't really trust him to care for the children. Besides, Denise worked thirty hours a week as a nurse and finances were tight.

Things hadn't always been this way for Leslie and Denise. They'd met when he was twenty-two and she was twenty-one. Leslie had not long been released from jail, where he'd served three years for break-and-enters and car stealing. He was unemployed and his life seemed aimless. Meeting Denise was a godsend, as she was very forgiving in regard to his difficult history. She was finishing her nursing training and probably took Leslie on as a bit of a project, to save him from his past and his failings and get him on the straight and narrow—she liked taking care of people. Her parents were not too pleased with her choice of partner, but in time they also warmed to Leslie and could see how he was blossoming under Denise's influence. In any case, Denise became pregnant after they'd been together for a year and a half, and the wedding went ahead within another three months.

Leslie doted on Denise. For the first time in his life, he felt loved and cared for. He willingly went to work (also for the first time in his life), labouring as a concreter and later driving a delivery truck. Denise appreciated his efforts and continued to provide emotional support, in a sense being the good mother he'd never had. Three children came along: two daughters and a son. At the time of Leslie's assessment by Dr Webber, the girls were aged eighteen and sixteen, and the boy fourteen.

Things began to unravel after Leslie suffered his serious back injury twelve years into the marriage. Years of hard physical work had taken their toll on Leslie's spine, and one day when he was lifting a heavy box, his back went. He developed severe sciatica and became disabled. Two operations helped relieve the leg pain but the back pain worsened. Before long, he was relying on powerful medication as much to soothe the emotional pain as the physical pain.

Leslie spiralled into a state of chronic pain, misery, pessimism, and rage against the world. Those closest to him bore the brunt of his resentment about his situation. The marriage, which had been such a support, steadily deteriorated. The children felt they no longer knew their father and withdrew in confusion and fear. Leslie was often verbally abusive over minor matters, and sometimes threw things around in frustration. At times, Denise feared he might assault her or the children.

Leslie's irritability and despair worsened into thoughts of hopelessness and suicidal ideas. He withdrew even more into his bedroom, and into a dark place in his mind. After the hope of release from his pain through surgery dissolved, the suicidal ideas and thoughts translated into plans, then actions. He took overdoses of his medication, sometimes washed down by rum, and ended up in hospital on a few occasions. There was a strong element of a 'cry for help' in his overdoses, as they generally happened in such a way that he was found before it was too late.

Lurking beneath this sad deterioration and Leslie's inability to adjust to his very difficult circumstances was the legacy of his upbringing. His family had been very dysfunctional. As a child, he was degraded and abused by his parents, who were alcoholic— much later, they would both die of cirrhosis of the liver. His father was very violent, especially when drunk, and would whip Leslie, his siblings and his mother. She struggled to care for the children, but she too was violent when she'd drunk too much cheap wine, which was often the case. Leslie had no safe haven and became an insecure, angry child. His two older sisters did most of the home care but they were no substitute for proper parents and themselves were abused. Leslie's older brother left home at fifteen and made his feelings known by changing his name.

Leslie reacted to the problems at home like many boys do in the same situation. He truanted from school, spending the day in parks on his own or with similarly aggrieved boys. He ran away from home several times, but he never got far and usually suffered a beating from his father after being returned home by authorities. There were some inquiries from the government children's service agency, but his father was very good at covering up.

Inevitably, from the age of about twelve, Leslie was in trouble with the police. At first, he shoplifted and stole from houses to get money or food when he was hungry. Then he and his peer group vandalised their school. Leslie started a couple of fires for the fun of it. It became evident to all concerned that he was out of control and that his parents were incapable of managing him. He ended up in boys' homes and juvenile detention, where he was again beaten and abused. He spent most of his adolescence in that environment, graduating to adult prison at eighteen and spending the next three years in custody for stealing property and cars. The courts had clearly decided that probation or community service wasn't going to work for this young man.

It was therefore a major turnaround in Leslie's life when he met Denise at a pub and she saw something in Leslie that others had not. For years the relationship had worked well, but then it unravelled when Leslie's back gave way, exposing the deep insecurity and shaky self-esteem that were a legacy of his childhood. He could no longer keep his side of the bargain in their marital relationship, and disillusionment and despair set in on both sides.

Earlier on the evening that Leslie was brought to the hospital and seen by Dr Webber, Denise had come home tired from an eight-hour shift spent caring for elderly demented patients. She wanted nothing more than to put her feet up. Her two daughters were having a sleepover with school friends, so it was just Leslie and their teenage son at home. She had some vague hope that Leslie might have prepared a meal and done the washing, giving her time to help her son with his homework before unwinding in front of the TV. But it proved to be a forlorn hope. Leslie had done nothing all day—none of the obvious household chores had been touched. He hadn't even showered, remaining slumped in front of the TV, looking miserable. Denise knew that if she confronted him, it was likely he would have one of his increasingly frequent temper tantrums. But she was too tired to care.

She told Leslie he was useless and things quickly degenerated into a loud argument. Leslie was furious, again accusing Denise of having no idea what he was going through. But Denise told him that things couldn't go on this way, that he had to get his act together and help her. Leslie said she was probably having an affair because she wasn't showing him any affection—he might as well be dead, as he wouldn't be able to cope if she were to leave him. Denise said he was being ridiculous. When would she have time for an affair? One thing was certain, though. He wasn't the man she'd married. She said she now had four children in the house instead of three.

Leslie started to sob and said that if she felt that way, he would make things simple for her and kill himself. Next thing, he'd locked himself in the bedroom and was rummaging through drawers and cupboards, looking for tablets to overdose on, all the while ranting and raging about how things had come to an end. This kind of talk had become familiar to Denise, but she knew Leslie would be serious about overdosing and she'd already hidden his medication after the last episode. Still, she had no idea what he might do when he couldn't find any pills, so she decided to call the ambulance. By the time the paramedics arrived, Leslie had stopped shouting and was sitting on the floor of the ensuite bathroom, crying.

The situation that Dr Webber now had to deal with was similar to the circumstances that had presented previously and for which Leslie had been repeatedly assessed, briefly admitted on two occasions, and was now seeing a psychiatrist. He had been prescribed an antidepressant, which calmed him and reduced his distress, but it could not take away the feeling that his life had spun out of his control. Previous assessors had made a formal diagnosis of an adjustment disorder with anxiety and depressed mood, with the obvious life stressor being Leslie's back problems, but with a major contribution being severe underlying personality vulnerabilities. His awful early life had left him with unresolved dependency needs and made it difficult for him to trust others to reliably care for him. He had been OK while his work and marriage went well, but as those two major planks in his life gave way, so did his emotional integration, shattering his former coping strategies. He simply had no idea how he was going to find his way out of this hole.

Dr Webber took a careful history to exclude indications of a more profound biological depression. It can be hard to distinguish between a severe depressive reaction to a life situation, and a biological depression caused by biochemical changes in the brain but possibly triggered by environmental stress. The latter condition could progress to psychotic depths, with a loss of contact with reality, depressive delusions, even voices telling the person how evil they are. Such a condition is very likely to lead to suicide, sometimes with others harmed as well in a murder–suicide, so it was important to work out if Leslie had any indications of it, which would require urgent inpatient treatment. Dr Webber couldn't find any such symptoms. That didn't mean Leslie's condition was not of serious concern, but it did mean that physical treatments such as antidepressants, mood stabilisers, antipsychotics or even ECT were unlikely to be the definitive answer for him. His reaction to events was in a way understandable, once all of the various contributing factors were taken into account. Management of the problem would involve helping Leslie with pain control, giving him strategies to deal with his distress, and assisting him and Denise in trying to find their way forward. Leslie's psychiatrist would provide support and psychotherapy, but other professionals would be important in dealing with pain and rehabilitation.

Dr Webber's task that evening boiled down to making an assessment of the risk attached to Leslie and of his immediate needs—the other management processes had been discussed with Leslie many times and were already in train. Dr Webber had to judge whether it was safe to release Leslie, or whether he needed to be admitted to hospital for his own safety or the protection of others, primarily Denise and the children. In the back of Dr Webber's mind was the fact that the nurses had told him there were no vacant beds in the inpatient unit. If Leslie needed to be in hospital, he would have to be transferred to another hospital, where he wasn't known, and that would be a difficult and time-consuming process. The shortage of beds was an issue that registrars on duty constantly had to deal with. It was never an easy task to persuade a hospital in a different catchment area that they should allocate one of their precious beds to a patient who should by rights be cared for in their own regional hospital. Dr Webber tried not to let these considerations colour his assessment of whether Leslie should stay in hospital or go home to community care.

By the end of the consultation, Leslie was far more composed. He'd stopped crying, and said he'd overreacted to the situation at home. He had been very angry with Denise, but in a way he could see her point of view. He'd done nothing to help that day. She was working to support him and he needed to be more understanding and try to do more. He loved Denise and hated it when she disapproved of him. It had been stupid of him to want to overdose, but he didn't feel that way now. He just wanted to go home and apologise to his wife, and he'd be happy to see his psychiatrist for his scheduled appointment in a few days.

Leslie agreed that he had a temper problem, that he had a short fuse these days, that sometimes he shouted and verbally abused Denise and the kids. A couple of times he had thrown things, and once he'd punched a wall. But he had not been violent to Denise and she never seemed frightened of him. Dr Webber phoned Denise to check the account of earlier events, and that she'd never seriously thought that Leslie would attack her. She confirmed this, but she also said Leslie's temper was an issue that disturbed her and the children. She would contact his psychiatrist if she had any serious concerns.

Dr Webber then phoned the psychiatrist on call, who was fairly familiar with Leslie's history, and gave her his assessment. There had been an acute crisis at home against a background of ongoing serious adjustment problems, but after a long talk, Leslie had settled and was no longer expressing any suicidal intent. He wanted to go home, and assured Dr Webber he would not harm himself or anyone else. Admission to hospital did not appear necessary and a follow-up had already been organised. The psychiatrist commented that, given the bed situation, it was just as well Leslie didn't need admitting, and after asking a few clarifying questions, she concurred with the management plan Dr Webber had outlined.

Leslie was discharged to go home. A taxi was called, and Denise was informed he was on his way. She had no way of knowing that she would soon be dead.

When Leslie arrived home, he went straight to Denise. He wanted her to hug him and tell him everything would be all right, that she would support him and love him and they would sort things out together. He thought he'd shed a few tears and apologise for his behaviour, then tell her that one day things would be as they were in the distant past, before his back gave way. But when he went into the kitchen, Denise kept her back to him as she stacked the dishwasher. He said, 'Hello, I'm back', but still she didn't turn around, and he felt tension rising in his chest. When she finally turned around, her face was set in a grim expression. She didn't look angry, she wasn't tearful, she was just determined. Leslie couldn't remember her ever looking like that before and it unsettled him. The tension in his chest turned into alarm.

Then Denise spoke. This time, she said, she'd had enough. Leslie had threatened to kill himself and taken overdoses so many times, and she had always forgiven him and tried to move on. But she felt blackmailed by his behaviour. He'd been trying to force her to love him, but in reality, with each suicide attempt she'd felt more distant, more alienated, less able to love him, more resentful and hopeless about their marriage. Now she'd realised it was over. There was no repairing the train wreck their life together had become. While he'd been at the hospital, she'd made the decision to leave him. Tomorrow, the children would not be coming home from school. Denise's father would pick them up and take them to their grand-parents' place. She would be packing her things in the morning and would be gone by the end of the day. He would have to face reality and fend for himself, grow up, sort himself out. He could talk to his mental health team about what he needed, but she was no longer able to help. It was now beyond her.

As Denise spoke, Leslie felt everything had become unreal. Her voice sounded strangely flat, as if she were speaking at a distance. It was as if he were looking at a movie rather than reality. Peripheral events seemed to become distant too. He was only dimly aware of the sound of a computer game coming from the lounge room, where his son was sitting. He could only try to focus on Denise's lips as they said things he couldn't believe she'd ever say. His face became flushed, he felt hot. An intense feeling of panic rose within him, mixed with the greatest sense of rage he'd ever experienced. He started to scream incoherently, as if an abscess in his mind had burst and all the horrible bile that had built up since his childhood was pouring out. He saw himself grabbing a large carving knife from a wooden block on the kitchen bench. He started stabbing Denise: once, again, then again and again, even after she'd fallen onto the floor.

Then he saw his son, standing there, watching in disbelief, and it stopped him. Suddenly, it all became real. There was blood everywhere. Denise gave a soft involuntary moan as she breathed out for the last time. Leslie fell onto his knees and began to sob as he'd never done before, saying, 'Oh God, no, Denise, I'm sorry, I'm sorry!'

The son called triple zero and an ambulance and the police were there in ten minutes. Leslie went into a paddy wagon and was taken to the Brisbane watchhouse, while the boy was taken to his grandparents, where his sisters would join him. The autopsy would show that Denise had been stabbed twelve times in the frenzied attack, with one of the wounds lacerating her heart, another severing her aorta, and others causing the collapse of her lungs.

The news filtered back to the hospital the next morning, when the Forensic Mental Health Service court liaison clinician rang to tell them that one of their patients had been charged with murder. The clinical director summoned Dr Webber and the psychiatrist who'd been on call the night before, to find out what had transpired. They were shocked to hear the news, especially Dr Webber. He'd never had a patient commit suicide while under his care, let alone murder his wife right after being assessed as presenting a low risk of violence. The psychiatrist, while distressed by the news, was a little more sanguine, knowing that predicting murder is an almost impossible task and no clinician can prevent every such tragedy. Like most psychiatrists, despite her best efforts, she'd lost some patients on her watch, but comforted herself with the knowledge that she'd prevented many more tragedies through the application of her training and skills. She was going to try to support Dr Webber during this crisis, and arranged to see him for more debriefing and supervision.

The clinical director did not overtly point a finger of blame, but he was clearly worried about what the media would report and how the hospital hierarchy and Queensland's minister of health would react. He was looking down the inevitable tunnel of inquiries, clinical post-mortem meetings and root-cause-analysis reports. He asked for a written report from both Dr Webber and the psychiatrist. It was important that each of them was careful to document everything, in case they were called as witnesses in a subsequent corner's inquest or murder trial. It was also likely that a request for an urgent ministerial report would closely follow media reporting of the circumstances of the murder.

Leslie was interviewed by police in the watchhouse. He did not want a lawyer present. His memory of the actual stabbing was clouded but, while sobbing intermittently, he admitted what he'd done. He said he'd completely lost control when Denise said she was leaving, as he couldn't face the future without her. He hadn't planned to kill her, had never wanted to do such a thing, but something took hold of him. It was as if he saw himself stabbing Denise but was unable to stop. He also asked how the children were and was assured they were being taken care of by their grandparents. Mostly, however, he talked about how awful things had been for him.

Leslie was charged with murder. He was granted legal aid and his lawyer sought a psychiatric report. Here was a man with an established psychiatric history. He'd been diagnosed with a depressive condition on top of his back problems and the damage to his family life. He'd been taking an antidepressant and seeing a psychiatrist. He'd made a number of suicide attempts, the last only a week ago. And he'd been seen at a hospital just before the killing due to further suicidal intent. The psychiatrist told Leslie's lawyer that there were strong grounds for believing that Leslie was impaired in his capacity to control his actions and fully comprehend the wrongfulness of his behaviour at the time of Denise's death. His case was therefore referred to the Mental Health Court for consideration.

The court ordered two more psychiatric assessments, which agreed with the first in that Leslie was impaired by his psychiatric condition to a substantial extent. The court's judgment was that Leslie was not completely deprived of capacities, so a defence of unsoundness of mind was not available to him, but he was sufficiently impaired by his illness to have suffered diminished responsibility at the time of the killing. This had the effect of reducing the charge from one of murder to one of manslaughter. Leslie then went on to plead guilty in the mainstream Supreme Court and he was sentenced to eight years imprisonment.

From prison, Leslie wrote a letter to his children telling them he was very sorry for what had happened. He hoped they would forgive him and he would try to be a better father to them in the future. They didn't respond. It was doubtful they would ever really forgive or understand Leslie. He had robbed them of their mother, but for a long time prior to that he hadn't been a real father to them anyway. Denise's parents now had to care for them, and they told the children that it would be best to forget their father. They couldn't forgive Leslie themselves, and they didn't believe the children should ever do so either. Leslie sent birthday and Christmas cards for a couple of years, but heard nothing in return. After that, he tried not to think of his children, although in the back of his mind he hoped that one distant day, when they'd grown up, he might be able to see them again.

Leslie settled back into prison remarkably quickly after so many years. The routine suited him. He didn't have to think about everyday demands. He had his own room, three meals a day, and other men to talk to and play cards with. After a short time, he was employed on light duties in the kitchen. He had no problem with the prison officers. He was polite and helpful, always dressed and ready for the unlocking of his door in the mornings, kept his room clean, and looked after his hygiene.

Leslie's depression seemed to lift surprisingly quickly, although the prison mental health service continued his antidepressants. It only took a few months for his grief and sadness to dissipate and for his sleep to settle. He had some nightmares about blood and violence, but they gradually became less frequent and then stopped altogether. The thing that most surprised Leslie, however, was the improvement in his back. The prison doctor told him they weren't willing to prescribe the narcotic painkiller he'd been taking at home, as it was too popular in prison as a drug of abuse. So he had to be satisfied with some short-term anti-inflammatory tablets and simple paracetamol. Leslie was upset about this and wondered how he'd cope, but his fears proved unfounded. He had some nausea and agitation for the first week after he stopped taking the painkiller, but after that his mind seemed a lot clearer and the pain was quite manageable. He followed the medical advice he was given and regularly walked around the prison oval, and he was careful not to do any heavy lifting or repetitive bending. He was never completely free of some backache, but it was not debilitating. It began to dawn on him that he'd been emotionally dependent on the narcotic medication and it had probably played a significant role in the difficulties he'd had coping with life in the years leading up to the killing of Denise.

Leslie eventually became a bit of a mentor and role model for the younger prisoners. He avoided getting involved with the trouble-makers. As a convicted killer, he tended to be left alone by those prisoners who were intent on the manipulation or domination of other inmates. Murderers have a certain perverse status in the prison environment, and it mattered little to inmates that Leslie's conviction was for manslaughter rather than murder. The prison authorities soon regarded Leslie as a model prisoner. His classification quickly progressed from 'high secure' down to 'low secure', which meant he could move from the large secure unit to the residential section. There, he shared a semi-independent area with five other low-secure prisoners.

Life seemed to be pretty easy, and Leslie was feeling better than he had for years. Three years into his sentence, he did develop severe blockages in three coronary arteries and underwent triple coronary artery bypass surgery, but a couple of weeks later he was able to return to his unit and slowly resume exercising.

Another development gave Leslie a further fillip. A mate of his in prison, who was serving a sentence for fraud, was being visited by his ex-wife, Doreen, aged forty-seven, with whom he remained platonically friendly. The man had been Doreen's second husband, the abusive first one having gone his own way years before. He spoke to Doreen about Leslie, saying he was basically a good man who was lonely, having no visitors. Doreen then wrote to Leslie and they became pen pals. She soon offered to visit Leslie, and in no time she started coming to the prison every week, and the relationship blossomed. The couple began to talk about a possible future together, believing they could love each other. Leslie now found himself feeling a lot more confident about a happy future life after prison.

Halfway through Leslie's sentence, prison authorities were so happy with him that they began to grant him day release and then weekend release, as part of a gradual progression to community release. They thought the new relationship with Doreen was a positive development, giving Leslie somewhere to go on his days out, and that influenced their decision-making. It wasn't long before Leslie and Doreen decided that they wanted to marry. Leslie approached the prison for permission and within a year of him meeting Doreen, it was granted. The simple wedding was presided over by a celebrant during a weekend release, in the garden of Doreen's rented cottage. Seven months later a baby girl was born, named Jasmine.

In 1997, six years into his sentence and now a remarried man with a baby daughter, Leslie commenced work release. He got a job at a warehouse doing despatch work, and received good reports from his employer. Things with Doreen were reportedly also going well. So Leslie was allowed to leave prison, with the remaining period of his sentence to be served as home detention and then on parole.

Prison romances are a peculiar thing, often more wishful thinking than reality, both partners blind to each other's failings. The relationship begins at a distance, usually by letter, then involves a prison visit for an hour or two a week, with phone calls in between. Each person imbues their partner with a rosy glow of promise, that of a new start. They do share facts about their pasts: the offences that led the man to prison, the broken marriages and domestic violence that made the woman feel bereft enough to look in a prison for someone to rescue her. But the man has learned his lesson, turned over a new leaf. He is only looking for love with a new woman who is prepared to forgive his past, accept him and care for him. And the woman, a one-time victim of abuse, is now looking for a strong man to care for her and accept her flaws, perhaps someone who can be the father figure her own destructive father never was.

But neither person really knows the other as a real human being. They only know the construct they have conjured. After the prisoner's release, it usually doesn't take long for each person's sharp edges to emerge, and they find themselves with someone they don't really know and possibly don't even like. Worse, they can find themselves reliving past relationship nightmares, feeling the same sense of disillusionment, and developing the same depression and substance-abuse problems they thought they'd left behind.

Leslie and Doreen's relationship followed this sadly predictable trajectory. Leslie was appalled to find that Doreen was not even a pale reflection of Denise. He saw her as lazy—she didn't work, was a poor housekeeper, and was only too happy to hand over the cooking and child care to Leslie while she chain-smoked and watched her daytime TV romances. He also discovered that Doreen liked to drink, and that her intake of cheap white wine was in inverse proportion to her contribution to household duties. Leslie then had to give up his job and go onto social security. His back pain had worsened, and his new GP seemed happy to put him back on his old narcotic painkiller. Money became increasingly tight, as the bills for grog and cigarettes and medication increased.

Doreen had a few girlfriends who had similar tastes in wine and more and more she would party with them late into the night, leaving Leslie to mope and take care of Jasmine. The silver lining was that he bonded with Jasmine as he had never done with his three other children, and she became the main reason he kept trying to make things better in the household.

Six months after Leslie had been released to home detention, Doreen announced that her stepson from her first marriage, 28-year-old Tom, was coming from interstate to stay with them. Leslie had no say in the matter, and the tension between him and Tom quickly became evident. Tom was just as lazy as Doreen and had a very cosy relationship with his stepmother. They drank and laughed together, ignoring Leslie and expecting him to do all the housework. Tom was also a pothead who spent much of his time stoned, and Doreen started using marijuana with him. To Leslie they seemed secretive and conspiratorial. He began to believe they might actually be having an incestuous sexual relationship. At one point he accused them of this, but they just laughed in his face, although they refused to deny it.

Leslie was furious about the drug use and suspected that Tom, with Doreen's help, was dealing pot to pay for their own consumption. He and Tom almost came to blows several times. Leslie didn't touch illicit drugs, but he compensated for that by increasing his dependence on his narcotic medication—once again, he was using it to treat emotional pain. His GP became so alarmed by the quantities of painkiller Leslie was consuming that he prescribed him methadone to deal with the dependence. The situation was rapidly spiralling out of control.

It was about three months before the eighth anniversary of Denise's death that things came to a head. Doreen and Tom stayed up late one night drinking and smoking, laughing and whispering. Leslie fed and bathed Jasmine and put her to bed before retreating to the main bedroom, feeling morose and alone. Doreen didn't come to bed that night, and the following morning, Leslie decided she'd spent the night with Tom. He found Doreen in the kitchen, in her panties and a T-shirt, boiling the kettle, cigarette dangling from her lips, looking the worse for wear. She looked at him but didn't speak.

Leslie told her he was sick of her treatment of him, and Jasmine deserved better too. Doreen was spending most of their money on drugs and grog and there was hardly enough left to buy baby food. Things would have to change. Nor would he tolerate her relationship with Tom for one more day. Tom would have to leave the house.

Doreen just looked at Leslie, no longer hiding the contempt she felt for him. He'd been a huge disappointment to her—not the strong man she'd wanted but a weak sop. She told Leslie that he was to leave Tom alone, that if he tried to get rid of him, she would take steps to have his parole cancelled. She could easily have him taken back to prison, and if that happened, he would never see his precious Jasmine again.

Later, Leslie would tell police he just lost it. While Doreen had been speaking, he'd felt weak, confused, cornered, desperate to keep Jasmine. But then his anger had taken over. His vision narrowed and things began moving in slow motion. He could see his hands around Doreen's neck, tightening, harder and harder. Her protruding tongue was purple and swollen and she couldn't speak. Her eyes bulged and bled. Then her bowels evacuated and she was on the floor, motionless.

Leslie was trembling as he stepped backwards, staring and panting. Suddenly, the house was deathly quiet. No sign of Tom or Jasmine—they had slept through it all. For Leslie, it was the start of another nightmare, another dead wife. He thought about whether he should just kill himself and put an end to everything, but then Jasmine called 'Daddy' and he knew he had to live for her. He picked up the phone, rang triple zero, and told the operator he'd killed his wife.

It was after this second killing that I was ordered to assess Leslie for the court. At that point, he'd been in the remand prison for several months and had again settled into familiar routines. He was back at work doing some light cleaning in the officers' dining room. He was still housed in the secure unit but hoped that after his trial he'd be able to get back to residential again, in the same prison where he'd served his previous sentence. There was no evidence of any psychotic disorder. In fact, the doctor at the prison had stopped Leslie's antidepressant, as there seemed no need for it, and he hadn't noticed any change. He was also off the painkillers and coping with his back pain through exercise and paracetamol.

During the interview, Leslie, who appeared to be of average intelligence, was relaxed and affable. He told me the whole sad saga of his life. The only good bits had been the early stages of his two relationships, especially with Denise, when there seemed to be some promise of emotional security and reliable love. But when things went bad, he couldn't face being abandoned and rejected. The most marked feature of the interview, however, was Leslie's lack of any real remorse for Doreen's murder. Instead, he presented all kinds of self-justifications, placing the blame on her and Tom for goading him into doing what he did. There was some lingering remorse for Denise's death—he felt somewhat responsible for that—but towards Doreen he just felt anger and bitterness. He seemed curiously lacking in insight into his own perceptions and had an entitled attitude as to the outcome of his coming trial. He expected that he'd receive a defence of diminished responsibility once again and that the court would have sympathy for the ordeal he'd been put through.

My assessment was that, at the time of Doreen's murder, Leslie was in a situational crisis, had adjustment difficulties, was reliant on methadone, and had dependent and antisocial personality traits stemming from a very bad early life. But there was insufficient evidence of a clinical disorder that would provide any psychiatric defence. Leslie had had plenty of life problems and understandable emotional reactions, but these did not amount to a psychiatric diagnosis. Other psychiatric opinions concurred, and Leslie, no doubt to his surprise and consternation, was found guilty of Doreen's murder and received a sentence of life imprisonment, with a minimum of twenty years to be served before being eligible for parole.

What lessons can be learned from this sad tale of serial wife murder? One lesson is that murder can be recurrent. It is rarely so, and the risk of such a repeat is therefore often not on the radar of probation and parole officers, nor of mental health professionals. But in this case, the risk factors that resulted in Denise's murder were still relevant and became critical as the relationship with Doreen began to fail. Leslie's personality was just as disordered and vulnerable, his needs still as they had been when he'd killed Denise. It was not as if he'd suffered a major illness that had been treatable after Denise died. If that were the case, the treatment would have probably kept him well, and protected Doreen. Unfortunately, the facts were more dangerous.

Leslie was still vulnerable to emotional chaos. Doreen was herself very troubled, with fewer strengths than Denise, and her marriage to Leslie was very likely to fail, as had her first two marriages. Leslie was almost certainly going to be left disillusioned and angry. It was a recipe for disaster that wasn't recognised as such at the time. Only hindsight can tell us that. Of course, while hindsight can be a good teacher, murder is such an infrequent occurrence that few of us have enough experience to be infallible when it comes to realising the full import of events as they unfold before our eyes. In this case, it was evident that psychiatrists, prison authorities, parole officers and family members were all fallible.

There had been enough evidence of a psychiatric disorder to gain Leslie a partial defence for his first murder, but not for his second. It can be a fine judgment as to whether a psychiatric defence is available when the charge is murder. Where the issues are related to personality and the effects of life events on a person's ability to cope, those judgments are particularly difficult. When does human suffering and emotional turmoil become pathological enough to make a formal diagnosis of psychiatric disorder? The two different decisions in Leslie's case illustrate the difficulties involved for assessors and courts. The judgments in the first case might easily have been less lenient, and a murder conviction would probably have prevented another murder down the track. But such a rare occurrence and tragic outcome cannot discount the validity of similar findings in the vast majority of other cases that do not have the same sad result as this one. Most judgments of diminished responsibility lead to the rehabilitation of the offender and a positive outcome for the community. Leslie's case gives all people working in the forensic field cause to think again about risk, and try harder in the future to make the right decisions.

We can never be perfect, however, and it would be unreasonable for the wider community to expect that. Errors in systems and risk assessment decision-making processes need to be addressed if they are clearly present, but scapegoats should not be found to appease the community's collective conscience every time things go wrong. Every such disaster should not necessarily lead to condemnation of the courts and stricter law enforcement measures, even if the media and the public demand it. The community agencies can do their best, but human frailty will always result in a baseline level of offending that no-one can totally prevent.

Leslie represented a case of enraged murder, the inhibitions controlling his killer instinct overwhelmed by a flood of fury. Murder resulting from out-of-control rage is probably the commonest type. It is also overwhelmingly a male problem—violence is mostly carried out by men—which has all kinds of complex evolutionary, genetic, hormonal and social origins.

An enraged murder is not the act of a confident man. Rather, it is like the other side of the coin that has defensive murder on it. It is about a man who needs to feel in charge and in control, especially over his partner. He has underlying insecurities and inadequacies that are often disguised by narcissism and hyper-masculinity. He tends to be jealous. There is often a history of domestic violence. He would never admit it, but he is also a dependent man, threatened by any hint of rejection, abandonment or loss of face. If his partner threatens to leave him, or if she does so, he will be terrified, but he'll experience that terror as rage. He will commonly seek to douse his anxiety with alcohol or drugs, as a form of self-medication. That usually only makes the situation worse, lighting the fuse that triggers an explosion.

What such a man then does with that rage will depend on a range of different factors. One will be whether he has grown up to believe that violence solves problems. He may have seen his father deal with things in that way. The behaviour of his peers might have strengthened that belief. His instinctive reaction might therefore be to attack. If he is handy with his fists. he might use those. If a weapon is within reach, that could be brought into play. Kitchen knives are never far away. Strangulation is always an option, even for a weaker man.

Men who are very dependent may not have the narcissistic mas-culine persona. Rather, they may be in a relationship where they are dominated and controlled by their partner, submissive and sub-servient. But they will also be acutely vulnerable to abandonment, and in the right circumstances, and with sufficient provocation, they too can turn into enraged murderers, taking violent revenge for one too many humiliations in the only way that seems possible in the heat of the moment.

The most likely victims of enraged murder are the offender's partner or the rival lover who is seen as stealing them away. Like the defensive murder, enraged murder tends to be a one-off event, but it's often preceded by lesser degrees of violent assault against previous partners and the eventual victim.

Leslie was a dependent man who had many underlying vulnerabilities. His two murders unfortunately fit with a not uncommon pattern seen in criminal courts. By the time he is next released, presuming he does not die in custody, he will be much older and it is unlikely there will ever be a third victim.

10

HIS OWN SECRET WORLD

I first met Lloyd Fletcher in 2011 when I was asked to assess him for the Queensland Supreme Court, thirteen years after he'd been imprisoned on an indefinite sentence for horrendous crimes against women. The law required that he be assessed at a time when he would normally be eligible for parole if he'd been given a life sentence. The court could decide to continue his indefinite detention, or commute his sentence to life imprisonment, in which case he could apply for parole. My report was to address the risk of future offending. There was a huge amount of material to review before the interview. I needed to look particularly closely at the details of Lloyd's offending so many years earlier.

It was April 1997. The weather in Brisbane was quite balmy, winter still some way off, when Jenny went out one Saturday night with workmates from the supermarket where she worked on a checkout. She was only sixteen years old and still living with her parents and younger brother in Wynnum, a bayside suburb. Her parents weren't too keen on her going out to the clubbing district, but she was quite mature for her age and made her own decisions about her social life. She also had a fake ID that enabled her to get into nightclubs. Her workmates were all at least eighteen and they bought the alcohol.

Jenny was a little tipsy when she caught the last train home and alighted at Wynnum station at 1.30 a.m. on Sunday. She had four short blocks to walk before she was home, and she was looking forward to a long Sunday sleep-in. She was the only person to get off the train, and the platform seemed deserted. But then she noticed a middle-aged man standing in the shadows near the station exit. There was nothing remarkable about his appearance, but his presence there on the platform, having made no move to get on the train, made Jenny feel uneasy. She walked purposefully towards the exit, avoiding any eye contact with the man, but he asked for a light for his cigarette. He then said that he'd been expecting his sister to get off the train but she must have missed it. Jenny said she didn't have a light—she didn't smoke, 'sorry'. She stepped quickly through the exit gate and started across the car park, empty except for a single car, towards the street. No-one else was around.

For a few moments everything seemed to be all right and Jenny was pleased to be not far from home. But then suddenly the man was behind her, grabbing her by the arm. In his other hand he had a knife, which he held near her throat. When Jenny screamed, he punched her hard in the face and got her in a headlock. He told her to shut up and cooperate or she'd be dead. The man dragged her to the car and shoved her into the back seat, then tied her hands together with some rope. He started to grope under her skirt, his finger pushing into her vagina. Jenny screamed afresh, refusing to give in. Then he had his hands around her throat and she blacked out. When he released the pressure, she started to come around again and immediately screamed some more.

The next thing Jenny knew, she heard shouting and she was being pulled out of the car. Someone was holding her and telling her they had her, that the bastard wasn't going to take her. Punches were thrown. The man who'd assaulted her jumped into the car and started it. As he drove off, one of Jenny's rescuers smashed one of the car's windows while another managed to take note of the car's registration.

It turned out that three teenage boys had been walking home after a party when they'd heard Jenny's screams and come to her rescue. The boys knew that they'd saved Jenny from a probable sexual assault, but they did not realise that they had in fact saved Jenny from becoming the latest victim of a serial rapist and murderer. Their actions exposed a dreadful series of offences against women, all wrought by one man, but brought to a halt when Jenny was rescued that night.

It didn't take long for the police to catch up with Lloyd Fletcher and arrest him. The car with the broken window was registered to him, and he had left DNA evidence on the rope, on the knife that was in the car, and on Jenny. Police found Lloyd at his home in the same suburb where he'd attacked Jenny. He admitted taking her from the station, and he could recall punching her in the face, but he claimed not to remember any other details.

The police quickly realised that they knew Lloyd Fletcher well. He was now thirty-nine years old, but his criminal history went back to when he was a teenager. He'd committed a number of serious sexual offences over two decades in two states, spending all but five years of that time in prison. He'd never been out for long before attacking another victim.

Brisbane police had another reason to be satisfied with Lloyd Fletcher's apprehension. He'd been a major person of interest during the investigation ten years earlier into the widely publicised murder of a fifteen-year-old girl, Janet Phillips. It was only hours after she'd left a party in Mansfield, apparently in a distressed state after witnessing a fight, that her naked and mutilated body was found dumped near a motorway on the outskirts of the city. As Lloyd's car, or one like it, had reportedly been seen near the area, and because he was known to police for similar attacks on women in the past, he'd been a person of interest. He was interviewed and had consented to a blood test, though he denied having abducted Janet. Attempts were made to match DNA from Lloyd to that obtained from fragmentary sperm samples recovered from Janet's vagina at the autopsy. However, the DNA technology in 1987 was relatively unsophisticated and no match could be obtained. Also, Lloyd's parents provided him with an alibi. So police could proceed no further with their investigation into him, and he'd then disappeared interstate.

A decade later, however, the science of DNA had developed significantly, and the police wasted no time in sending a new DNA sample from Lloyd to the forensic laboratory. The forensic samples from the Janet Phillips case could now be re-examined using the new techniques. There was more than a little excitement among the cold case team when Lloyd's new sample was matched to the sperm taken from Janet.

Lloyd Fletcher had been charged with a raft of offences after the assault on Jenny—deprivation of liberty, assault occasioning bodily harm, disabling in order to commit rape, and attempted murder. Now he also found himself charged with the murder of Janet Phillips, which police believed represented one of the most serious and grotesque examples of recurrent offending by a violent sexual sadist.

Lloyd's earlier criminal history made for equally disturbing reading. It began before his fourteenth birthday with a charge of 'aggravated assault on a female'. This was legal jargon, usually decoded to mean an assault on a female, sometimes a very young female, with some implied sexual intent. Official records providing details of this offence were not available to me, but there was a brief mention elsewhere in the reams of material I had that it may have involved some kind of assault of a woman on a bridge in Innisfail in far north Queensland, where Lloyd then lived. When the case went to court, he was discharged into his mother's care, with no punishment. Lloyd would not tell me anything more, saying he'd put it out of his mind.

When Lloyd was fourteen-and-a-half years of age, an application for care and control was made and he was placed with Queensland's

Department of Children's Services. Clearly, his home environment was not coping with him. The records indicated that his parents had separated for a period of time at that stage and Lloyd had been taken to Brisbane by his mother, but he was then sent back north to his father. When the father was hospitalised with heart disease, Lloyd was cared for by a strict housekeeper until his mother returned to take over his care.

A year later, there was a further charge of aggravated assault of a female, associated with breaking into a house 'with intent'. The implication again was that there may have been a sexual motivation underlying Lloyd's behaviour. But at trial, no evidence was offered— it appeared the female victim did not wish to give any—and he was again placed into the care of Children's Services for a period of two years.

Sexually motivated assaults like this at such a young age are a cause for serious concern. They often presage an ongoing pattern of increasingly severe sexual offending in adult life. The records also showed evidence of other antisocial behaviour from a young age.

Just prior to turning seventeen, Lloyd was warned for unlicensed driving. Six months later, he was convicted of shooting several cows with a rifle. For that, he was sent to a juvenile detention centre for eighteen months. When I interviewed him, Lloyd was unable to tell me why he'd done such a thing, but I noted that he'd previously told a psychologist that he'd chosen to kill only heifers: young female cows.

Violence towards animals in childhood is generally seen as a possible predictor of later violence towards people, and the potential development of an antisocial personality disorder. Lloyd's deliberate choice of female cows could be seen as a specific predictor of women being the victims of his future violence.

There were more brushes with the law as soon as Lloyd was freed from detention, namely unlicensed driving, disqualified driving, stating a false name, and dangerous driving with a blood alcohol level of 0.08 per cent. That last episode earned him fines, the

absolute disqualification of his driver's licence, and fourteen con-
secutive weekends of detention. These were clear indications that
Lloyd was not able, nor willing, to live within the rules of society.

It was just prior to Lloyd's twentieth birthday that the first of his
serious sexual offences occurred. The official account was chilling.

In 1977, Cynthia, just twenty years old, was walking home from
evening netball practice in Innisfail, where she'd grown up. She had
just crossed the South Johnstone River on the Jubilee Bridge when
a man appeared from behind the pylons. He dragged her by the hair
off the footway and down an embankment. Cynthia screamed, but
the man covered her mouth and held a knife to her throat. He told
her to do as he said or he'd cut her throat. The man was strong, and
Cynthia could put up little resistance. He hauled her to a nearby
park where he pulled off her shorts and panties and raped her.

The man then ordered her to get dressed. Trembling, Cynthia
was doing so when, without warning, the man grabbed her by the
throat and choked her until she lost consciousness. She came to
on a narrow jetty on the river and began screaming, but the man
punched her hard twice in the mouth and again she blacked out.
The next time Cynthia came to, she was in the river with her bra
tightly knotted around her neck. It appeared that while she was
unconscious, the man had fixed the garment around her throat,
then thrown her off the jetty, along with her remaining clothes
and her handbag, and left the scene. But the cold water must have
shocked her awake. Somehow, Cynthia managed to struggle up onto
the riverbank. She could barely breathe, but the bra was so tightly
knotted that she couldn't get it off her neck. She stumbled though
mangroves to a nearby house, where a woman cut the bra off and
called the police. It was astounding that Cynthia had survived this
terrifying ordeal—her attacker had clearly not intended her to live
to tell the tale.

Lloyd was arrested while driving south on a highway after
leaving the scene of the attack. He'd been stopped for driving too
fast, then found to be intoxicated and unlicensed. Police suspected

he was Cynthia's attacker because a car like his had been spotted near the Jubilee Bridge, and he matched Cynthia's description of her assailant. Lloyd stood trial for rape and attempted murder. He was found guilty and sentenced to eight years and fifteen years, respectively, for those offences. However, after nine years out of circulation, Lloyd managed to get parole.

In July 1987, Janet Phillips, a Grade 10 student, had left a friend's party in Mansfield in the early hours of the morning to walk home, but she never made it. Within a few hours of her worried mother alerting police of Janet's disappearance, a report came in that the body of a young girl had been spotted by a man walking his dog near the Gateway Motorway, some five kilometres from Janet's last known location. She was found lying in a culvert at the bottom of a large embankment.

Investigators could immediately tell that terrible violence had occurred at the embankment, which could be accessed by a vehicle via a rough track. Janet's body was naked, buttons from her blouse and some jewellery lying nearby—her clothes were never found. She had bruises to her face and forehead, and genital injuries. It was surmised that the girl had been dragged down the embankment to the culvert, probably face down, then fatally stabbed four times in the upper body. The autopsy revealed that there were additional post-mortem slashes around the lower abdomen and vulval area, as well as around the left buttock, suggestive of some kind of depraved or sadistic ritual violence. Mud was found in the girl's vagina, possibly from the attacker trying to wash it out to remove traces of sperm. In that, he was not totally successful, as some degraded samples of sperm were recovered.

A witness reported a car similar to Lloyd's near the scene of the killing. They'd taken particular note of it because it was unusual to see vehicles in that location. Lloyd's history clearly made him a person of interest and he was subsequently interviewed. However, he denied being anywhere near the embankment at the time of Janet's murder, and without a clear match between his DNA and the degraded sperm samples, police did not have enough evidence with which to charge him.

Having avoided being charged with Janet's murder, Lloyd travelled to Victoria, where he got work as a builder's labourer. He was by then married for the second time, having met his wife while he was in prison. She'd previously been the de-facto partner of Lloyd's older brother, whom he had never got along with, and it had suited her to leave with Lloyd for another state to put some distance between her and her apparently violent former partner. She was relatively unconcerned about the fact that her new husband had himself just served a long sentence for rape and attempted murder, as Lloyd had been convincing in explaining to her that he was a reformed man.

For about a year and a half, things seemed to go quite well for the couple in their new environment, which allowed them both a fresh start. They rented a house in Bright, in northern Victoria. The town was in the foothills below some popular winter snowfields and had a nice community feel about it. But then, in 1990, Lloyd was charged with another serious assault. This time he was accused of kidnapping and recklessly causing injury.

Terri, a thirteen-year-old local girl, was cycling home one afternoon after her school's sports day. She lived with her family on the edge of Bright, and the cycle track that led home took her along a rather rough road through a forested area and over a single-lane bridge over a creek. As Terri cycled along the road, a car passed her, going in the same direction. She saw the male driver look at her but she didn't know him. She rode around a couple of bends and finally reached the bridge, which was about a kilometre from her home. As she rode across it, she saw the man who'd driven the car walking towards her from the other end of the bridge, holding a sheath knife. The man reached her before she had time to turn around and pedal away, and he ordered her to get off her bike. Terri screamed and started to run, but she tripped and fell on the rough road, taking patches of skin off her knees and forehead. The man put the knife blade to her throat, and when Terri screamed again, he put his hand over her mouth. Then he told the terrified girl in a calm but firm voice to walk across the bridge.

As they got to the other end of the bridge, two cars approached. The man made Terri stand behind him, either to try to hide her or to pretend they were walking arm in arm. But somehow Terri was able to make eye contact with the driver of the second car and gestured with her hand to indicate she needed help. When the car stopped and its two young male occupants came towards them, Terri's attacker let go of her and ran off. The two men from the car pursued the man, and after he briefly threatened one of them with his knife, they cornered him. The man threw his knife into the scrub before being subdued. Police were quickly on the scene and arrested the man, whom they identified as Lloyd Fletcher.

At the trial, the judge scoffed at Lloyd's claim that he'd just wanted to talk to Terri. He saw evidence of planning on Lloyd's part, even if it was only brief. He also noted the similarity to Lloyd's previous attack on Cynthia in Innisfail, that in both cases the victim was on a bridge and threatened with a knife—although the judge was not aware of the much earlier assault, when Lloyd was thirteen, that also involved someone on a bridge. It seemed that that modus operandi was his way of trapping a victim, allowing them little means of escape. The judge sentenced Lloyd to a total of six years imprisonment. Once again, Lloyd Fletcher was in custody and young females were temporarily safe from his sadistic impulses.

He served four years of his sentence before being paroled and heading north to live in Brisbane. It was about three years later when his dark inner impulses took over once again and he attacked Jenny at the Wynnum train station. By that stage, he had seriously offended against at least four women over twenty years, beginning when he was nineteen years old. If the earlier adolescent offences with indications of sexual motivation were taken into account, it would extend the period of his known sexual offending to twenty-five years. He'd served a total of fifteen years in custody, but the time he'd spent locked away from society had made no difference to his dangerous sexual sadism. So there was no reason to believe that with the 1997 assault, he'd reached the end of his sexual offending.

At Lloyd's 1998 trial regarding the offences against Jenny, the judge noted that there was no indication of a relevant mental health defence. He also noted the extraordinary severity of Lloyd's offending. He had raped two women in the past and had intended to rape the most recent victim. All three women were threatened with a knife, dragged from a public place, and subjected to severe violence, leaving them with physical and emotional scarring. His most serious and disturbing offence was the murder of Janet Phillips, with indications of sadistic rape and the mutilation of his victim— Lloyd had been sentenced two months earlier to twenty years imprisonment for the rape, and life imprisonment for the murder. Unstated, but no doubt evident to the judge and all those in the courtroom, was the realisation that the two other victims might have met the same fate had they not been rescued.

The judge was convinced that Lloyd was a serious and long-term danger to the community. He noted that, even if the court were to impose a life sentence, the danger would persist even at the end of such a sentence, with vulnerable young women in isolated situations being at particular risk of Lloyd's lustful predations. The judge was drawn to the inevitable conclusion that the appropriate outcome was an indefinite sentence.

Thirteen years later, as I made preparations to interview Lloyd so I could provide my risk-assessment report, I understood that his criminal history spoke for itself. I was obviously going to look closely at the details of his offences to discern the precise nature of his sexual perversion, sadism and other motivations. But I was also keen to look at his childhood experiences to try to find out where all of this might have originated. Only then would I be able to really understand the subtleties of Lloyd's motivation and know whether any treatment options might be available. If he were not willing to give me such access to his inner life, a more generic, broad-brush assessment of risk would be all that was possible.

Lloyd appeared to be of average intelligence. He had a good vocabulary and was literate, his concentration and memory were normal, and he was very neatly groomed. He was a reserved and rather reluctant interviewee, but he showed no symptoms of any mental disorder, nor any obvious emotional distress.

When I explored the first major offence against Cynthia on the bridge in Innisfail, Lloyd claimed only partial recall but accepted his guilt. However, he tended to minimise the seriousness of his actions and denied any murderous intent. He said, 'I never thought she was dead. I didn't go that far.' He made various excuses for his behaviour, claiming he'd drunk two bottles of tequila that day. He'd been annoyed with his employer for making him go on a work trip up north during the week of his wedding anniversary and his daughter's birthday, and had dealt with his irritation by drinking every day of the trip with an alcoholic workmate. This indicated to me that he had poor coping skills, but none of his statements were sufficient to explain his violent, sadistic and potentially murderous behaviour towards a total stranger simply going about her normal life. There were clearly much darker and more perverse motivations involved, which Lloyd wouldn't or couldn't disclose.

He adamantly denied subsequent involvement in Janet Phillips' murder and said he would continue to do so until the day he died. He claimed the vehicle seen near the scene of the crime was different from his. He claimed the DNA evidence had been corrupted and that the laboratory worker involved was dismissed six months later for falsifying evidence in another case. (At the trial, Lloyd's defence lawyer had asserted that there'd been various improper practices in the DNA testing, but these were carefully refuted during cross-examination of the experts.) He even claimed that another prisoner had confessed to Janet's murder but that the authorities had 'told him to bugger off'. Given that he was denying all involvement in the murder, his motivations could not be explored. I was left with no

understanding of the feelings and drives that had led to an innocent
young girl being abducted, raped, murdered and mutilated.

I also asked Lloyd about his attempted abduction of Terri in
Bright. Again, he claimed only partial recall of what had happened.
He did say he'd been 'pissed off' that day because his boss had sent
him to work on his house and yard rather than on the building site
where Lloyd should've been employed. Also, he'd had an argument
with his wife the night before about some trivial matter, which he
could no longer remember. He claimed the knife he'd carried was
one he kept in his lunch box to peel oranges. But no explanation
was forthcoming for why he would assault and threaten a young
woman he didn't know. He gave no insight into what he was thinking at the time, or what his intentions were.

In regard to the attempted abduction of Jenny, he remembered
being upset at the time. After having stuck with him during and
after his prison sentence in Victoria for assaulting Terri, his second
wife had abruptly left him, and he was trying to work out why. Also,
his mother was ill in hospital, and he was annoyed with his younger
sister, who was sponging off him, wanting him to do everything
for her. On the night of Jenny's attack, he'd had a few drinks and
then gone out driving to think about things. He didn't tell me any
more about his motives or actions that night, just that he was glad
the girl got away.

Lloyd's medical history was unremarkable. He'd once had a
hernia fixed, and he'd received a head injury as a child that had led
to a few days in hospital. He had no history of any psychiatric disorder and was not taking any medication. He'd never thought about
self-harm, seeing suicide as 'the coward's way'. He'd also never had
cause to be assessed by a prison mental health service.

Lloyd had drunk alcohol quite heavily from the ages of fifteen
to seventeen, but after that, binges were rare. The only one of his
offences associated with significant alcohol intoxication was the one
involving Cynthia in 1977, when he claimed to have drunk a lot
of tequila at the climax of a week of drinking. However, he did not

believe he'd drunk that much in order to give him the courage to offend. He was a long-term moderate cigarette smoker. He'd tried marijuana only once, in his teens, and had never used any illicit drugs since—he had strong anti-drug attitudes. This was backed up by the fact that all the urine drug tests he'd taken in custody had been clear.

Both of his parents had died while Lloyd was in custody—his last visit from them had taken place thirteen years before I assessed him. Five years before our interview, his mother had suffered a fractured hip and succumbed to pneumonia, aged sixty-five. Lloyd described her as a very strict but caring mother, a good person who would do anything for her children. His father had lived to eighty-seven, dying of cancer two years earlier. He'd been a mechanic who had 'itchy feet' and moved his family from town to town, apparently chasing work. Lloyd said he was a quiet man, never aggressive. Neither parent abused alcohol, and there was no family history of any psychiatric disorder. Lloyd had six siblings: an older brother, four older sisters and one younger adopted sister. However, he'd had little to no contact with them in recent years, apart from a very occasional letter from one older sister.

While Lloyd's account of his childhood and family life was quite bland and featureless, my reading of extensive custodial reports indicated that there'd been a good deal more going on during his early years than he'd told me. His mother apparently had quite a temper and was said to have thrown things during arguments, notably flinging a knife at her husband on one occasion and causing some injury to his back. Lloyd minimised all this, although he agreed there had been some fights over silly things, and admitted his mother had hit him with a jug cord when he did anything wrong. But the fact that Lloyd had been placed under the care of the Department of Children's Services three times between the ages of thirteen and fifteen indicated there'd been serious problems with his behaviour, and suggested a much more dysfunctional home life than he was prepared to admit. In particular, there appeared to be some family secrets involving the father that Lloyd was not willing to accept.

After Lloyd was sent to prison for the attack on Terri, his second wife went to stay with Lloyd's parents. But that arrangement came to a sudden end when she accused Lloyd's father of trying to rape her. At first, Lloyd was very angry with his father and told him he'd never forgive him for what he'd done. However, his father denied that such an event had ever happened, and Lloyd's mother supported the father's story. Lloyd eventually came to believe that his wife had lied about what had happened as a ploy to extract herself from the household.

Another indirect indication of a secret involving the father was that after Lloyd's mother died, all of his siblings shunned the father. Lloyd thought this was wrong but he was never able to find out why they did it. He denied ever being the victim of any sexual abuse, and had no knowledge of any sexual abuse of his siblings, but I wondered if this could've occurred. Lloyd was also very vague about the reason why his father had moved the family around so many times when he was young. It may have been to find work, but I speculated that some aspect of the father's behaviour towards others might have resulted in him repeatedly running from trouble. The separation of the parents when Lloyd was thirteen also remained unexplained.

Lloyd wasn't particularly motivated as a student and was caned intermittently for not doing his homework. He also occasionally wagged school but was never suspended or expelled. At the end of Grade 8 he left school to work on a fishing trawler, around the time his parents separated and Lloyd started getting into legal strife. He worked on the trawler for a year before he went to juvenile detention, and his subsequent work history was severely compromised by repeated incarcerations. In prison, he completed an apprenticeship as an upholsterer but was never able to use that qualification in the community. During his relatively short periods of employment, he usually worked as a builder's labourer.

Lloyd had a series of girlfriends in his mid-teens. He became engaged to a girl when he was only fifteen, while he worked on the fishing trawler, but their relationship only lasted a year. Her father

was very controlling and pressured Lloyd to work with him in a
cane mill and to live in a flat he owned. The relationship was very
closely monitored, such that it never became sexual, and this parental
interference eventually broke the couple apart. Lloyd quickly found
another girlfriend with whom he was able to have sex, but they
soon went their separate ways. That was closely followed by several
other casual sexual relationships with local girls.

Lloyd met the woman who would become his first wife at a
riverside bar in Brisbane when he was seventeen, and before long
she was pregnant. Lloyd had been 'brought up to do the right thing',
so they married before their daughter was born. They lived together
for two years, and it appeared that Lloyd was reasonably committed
to that relationship. But then he went off on a work trip and, on
the cusp of their wedding anniversary, his shocked wife heard of his
arrest for the rape and attempted murder of a girl called Cynthia, a
complete stranger.

From prison, Lloyd suggested to his wife that she file for divorce,
as he wouldn't be released for many years. Surprisingly, she stood by
him, and they nurtured hopes of rekindling their relationship. In fact,
when Lloyd was released on parole after nine years, they had a one-
off sexual encounter. His wife soon said she was pregnant and that
Lloyd was the child's father, but he was doubtful. He spoke to me
quite disparagingly of his first wife, saying she'd had four children by
different fathers and four abortions. She eventually divorced Lloyd
and married a man who was 'a drunk, a woman basher and a child
basher'. His last contact with her was when she'd written to him
after his arrest thirteen years earlier, a letter he ignored. He did have
weekly contact by letter with his daughter, who was married to a
minister of religion, but he forbad her to visit him in prison and
had never had telephone contact with her.

Lloyd freely accused his first wife of failing to meet his expectations of a woman's standards of behaviour, while he was in prison
indefinitely for terrible offences against women. That hypocrisy
seemed indicative of some deeply embedded negative attitudes

towards women that might be very relevant to his offending. There was no hint of remorse for his betrayal of his young wife.

Lloyd met his second wife after he'd been incarcerated for the rape and attempted murder of Cynthia. The woman was, as mentioned, his older brother's de-facto partner, and had visited Lloyd in prison. Having hooked up and headed to Victoria together, their new life was shattered when Lloyd was arrested in Bright for attacking Terri. Just as his first wife had seen something in Lloyd that made her stick with him for a long time, the second wife stuck by him too, waiting for four years until he was released and then living with him again in Brisbane. The couple were reasonably happy for a couple of years, at least as far as Lloyd was concerned, but then his wife suddenly left him. Lloyd said this came as a big shock. He wondered if his wife's sister, who lived in Victoria, had somehow influenced her to return there, having never really trusted Lloyd because of his past offending. His anger towards his wife for what he perceived as her unjustified abandonment of him seemed to be the trigger for his assault on Jenny.

Lloyd told me he'd always had problems controlling his temper. He'd regularly get angry, often with little provocation. Even in prison, he got annoyed by incompetent prisoners who were under his supervision in the workshops. He said he expressed his anger verbally, or by withdrawing, rather than through physical violence, but sometimes after an angry outburst, he couldn't fully recall the events that had taken place. One such episode had occurred earlier in his life, when he'd consumed alcohol after being rejected by a girl and had come to in the morning with bloodied knuckles. He realised he'd smashed his fist into the glass of a petrol bowser at a nearby service station, but he couldn't remember why.

Despite these issues, Lloyd actually set very high standards for himself in terms of everyday behaviour. His prison record was good. He was very tidy and clean. A couple of small fights had occurred in the early years of his latest sentence, but he was mostly very settled, with an excellent work record.

When it came to close friendships, though, Lloyd had never been keen on them, having had little opportunity to experience them in his childhood because of constantly moving house. As an adult, he was a quiet loner, not a sociable man. Even in prison, he kept his contact with officers to the essentials only, and generally avoided any close associations. The one close male friendship he could recall had ended acrimoniously in 1987, when his friend gave evidence against him in court. So Lloyd tended to spend time alone, reading a lot. When I asked him what he liked to read about, Lloyd said he had a long-term interest in things to do with Germany. Closer questioning revealed he was interested in the politics of the 1930s and 1940s, and that he admired Hitler, considering him a good politician. He said that if he'd lived in Germany at that time, he would've joined the Nazi Party. He also liked reading novels about 'dungeons and dragons'.

Interestingly, Lloyd also told me he'd become a Buddhist around 1985, his initial interest piqued by lectures in prison given by a Buddhist monk. During his last period out in the community, Lloyd had met up with the monk again and ever since then had embraced the practice of meditation and yoga for up to two hours every day. He found those practices helpful in dealing with migraine headaches and petty prison politics. He also read Buddhist literature.

Sexually, Lloyd was firmly heterosexual and had refused approaches from men in prison. He indicated an attraction to 'mature females'. When asked what age he preferred for a partner, he said 'twenty-three', an oddly specific answer for a man in his mid-fifties. He denied any sexual interest in underage females and couldn't explain why three of his victims had been aged thirteen, fifteen and sixteen, respectively. He also emphatically denied any sexual interest in children, and in fantasies involving rape or bondage, or gaining sadistic pleasure from inflicting pain. His sexual drive was reported to be average.

Lloyd had generally refused educational opportunities in prison. A year before I saw him, he'd agreed to do an introductory sexual offender assessment program, but he felt forced to do this, and his attitude was distrustful. He apparently told the group that he would never be released from custody and had no intention of challenging the indefinite sentence when it came up for review. The course facilitators also reported that Lloyd had indicated he was aware of the danger he posed and had said that the community would be safer if he were kept in secure custody. But when I asked him about this, Lloyd denied having said that and accused the facilitators of distorting his words. He wanted their comments expunged from his record.

During the program, Lloyd did accept responsibility for his offences. The exception was the murder of Janet Phillips, for which he continued to maintain his innocence. He also ultimately deflected any focus on his offences and preferred it when the group was sympathetic to him in regard to his indefinite sentence. When he did talk about his most recent offence, against Jenny, he said 'it was lucky for her' that the teenagers had rescued her. But he showed little remorse for his offending, little ability to empathise with his victims, and a lot of difficulty in connecting with his own emotions. He had little interest in attending any further sexual treatment programs, and the facilitators expressed the view that his denial of Janet's murder, his lack of trust in therapeutic processes, and his reluctance or inability to access his inner emotional life, represented significant barriers to any further treatment.

It was certainly impossible for me to get Lloyd to really explain or explore the reasons behind his offending. He was able to say that his victims and his family had suffered immensely because of his behaviour, and that, as a result, he despised himself. He recognised that he'd done wrong, particularly in offending against underage females, and he therefore believed that he deserved to be in prison. But he couldn't actually think about his offences, let alone talk about them. Whenever he tried to do so, it made him physically ill, to the point of vomiting if he persisted in trying. He said, 'I don't want to look at that part of myself. I hate it.' He was simply resigned to spending the rest of his life in prison.

The closest Lloyd could get to defining the reasons for his actions was that it had to do with anger and disillusionment regarding women. Oddly, despite his unhappy experiences with women, he maintained that he still trusted them '70 per cent'. He also thought alcohol had contributed to his offending and he'd decided he would never touch it again. This contrasted with a previous statement that only his assault on Cynthia had been associated with intoxication. Perhaps his new assertion indicated that the murder of Janet Phillips had been associated with alcohol as well but, of course, Lloyd could not confirm that while maintaining his innocence for that offence.

From a clinical point of view, interviewing Lloyd was frustrating because I was given little opportunity to understand his motivations and inner emotional life. He was largely a closed book—no real rapport or connection was possible. My experience was similar to that of the psychologists who'd previously attempted to understand and report upon Lloyd's offending for courts or parole boards. They'd all found him similarly introverted and defensive. Like me, they had to fall back upon indirect indicators from his history to get hints as to the reasons why he'd become such a serious offender. His mother's aggression, the constant shifting between towns as a child, the unexplained parental separation, and the estrangement of his siblings from his widowed father—they were the main areas of focus. But I believed that these facts were insufficient to explain the monster within Lloyd who'd randomly carried out violent, sadistic crimes against innocent young women. There had to be much more that I didn't know.

The interplay of sadistic sexual violence, rape and murder is generally difficult to understand, mostly because those who commit these crimes are either unable or unwilling to help us do so. Milder forms of sadistic pleasure and the obverse, masochism, are not uncommon. Bondage and discipline as part of a normal sexual relationship is well recognised. But it is a consensual activity with clear limits on the extent of violence agreed to by both parties. The kind of sadism involved in sadistic rape and murder is totally different. The victim is most often unknown to the offender, at the very least not involved in a sexual relationship with them. The unsuspecting victim, who may have been chosen because of their age, appearance or simply availability, is often lured into danger or trapped in an isolated place. The violence is forced and extreme, and weapons and restraints can be involved. This violence may extend beyond what is necessary to subdue or even kill someone. There may be mutilation before or after death, carried out to fulfil a long-held secret fantasy.

Such terrible offences are usually preceded by years of preparation, with much mental rehearsal of precisely how events will unfold, accompanied by masturbation. The first few attempts may be fumbled and incomplete, but they become more closely realised in further episodes. Thus evolves the serial rapist or murderer. We know this is the common pathway, through observation of the offences and their repeated common features, and the particular modus operandi. We also know how the offender evolves in their mind and sexual drive, thanks to accounts given by those offenders willing to talk or cooperate in psychological therapy.

In Lloyd's case, I had to make assumptions about what his motivations were. But even without his cooperation, it was possible to make a diagnosis and recognise the risk of recurrence. His lack of cooperation actually heightened the risk of reoffending because it demonstrated he had not come to terms with the problem himself and wouldn't allow anyone else to help him understand and address his actions.

Lloyd Fletcher indicated that he hated the monstrous part of himself that allowed these offences to occur, and that attempting to talk or think about them made him physically ill. He claimed limited memory of certain details of the offending. It was possible that there were strong psychological defences at play, keeping the worst of the memories repressed. Dark and violent impulses might indeed have been 'ego alien' to him—not a part of himself that he could acknowledge. But it was also possible that he chose not to talk about what he'd done because it was his own secret world, to be enjoyed only by him, in private.

Serial murderers who claim amnesia may actually have kept trophies from the scene of the offence, such as a piece of clothing. Some are known to secretly return to the scene to once again experience sexual excitement and masturbate to the memories. It's likely that most such killers do in fact recall their crimes in great detail and love to relive them in fantasy.

Sadistic rape or murder tends to recur in cycles. The drive and pressure to offend builds up until an attack is triggered. The drive is discharged, temporarily satisfied, but then it starts to build up again until the monster within gets their way once more. All of this may occur behind an apparently normal facade of someone in a family, holding down a job, or interacting socially with friends and neighbours. Such extreme sexual violence clearly requires a melding of sexual drive and orientation with extreme anger. These factors are then likely to be linked to psychopathic personality traits involving a lack of empathy towards others and extreme self-centredness. The person's family and developmental history will often contain hints of what is to come. There will often be early neglect, physical and severe sexual abuse, and domestic violence. Antisocial personality traits may be inherited and then exaggerated by early trauma and abuse. But even these things do not often seem sufficient to fully understand the origins of severe sexual sadism. Many people come through very bad childhoods with an array of psychological baggage, but only a tiny minority become serial rapists or murderers. Whatever makes that difference in someone's life trajectory seems to me to be something of a mystery in most cases. Certainly, Lloyd's known history is not sufficient to understand why he became a repeat serious sex offender. Perhaps we will never know the truth about him.

The assessment I provided to the court was that, judging by the pattern of the offending, Lloyd Fletcher had the paraphilia of sexual sadism, although a definitive diagnosis of that condition was made difficult by the lack of history in regard to the subjective drives he experienced. Sexual arousal, rage towards women, and a wish to inflict pain and humiliation upon his victims, had led to homicidal impulses resulting in one murder and at least one other attempted murder, with two other victims rescued from a possible similar fate. The apparent post-mortem mutilation of Janet Phillips indicated an even more extreme sadistic paraphilia.

This sexual sadism occurred in a man with a personality disorder, with antisocial and schizoid traits. Formal assessment using the psychopathy checklist indicated that a diagnosis of psychopathic personality wasn't warranted, although there were some above-average psychopathic features, particularly in relevant areas such as difficulty in relating empathically to others. There was no indication of any other diagnosable psychiatric illness.

I took into account all of the background material I had read, my interview with Lloyd, and the results of formal risk-assessment instruments, before coming to the conclusion that he was a high-risk offender who would likely rape or murder again, and that such offending could well be recurrent and difficult to predict or prevent by supervision in the community. He'd refused to participate in an intensive sexual offender program in custody, and therefore both he and any future supervisor did not have the benefit of any insights that might've come from such a program. Under those circumstances, safe management in the community would not be possible. Increasing age would not be a significant preventive factor in the absence of treatment, and even if Lloyd did undergo treatment, there was no guarantee that the risk would be reduced to a safe level. Therefore, I considered continuing detention to be the only reasonable option.

The court determined that the risk to the community presented by Lloyd Fletcher could be managed only by continuing his indefinite sentence. It was not commuted to life imprisonment. As it was, Lloyd, through his lawyer, had not pressed for a change to his indefinite sentence.

Lloyd remains in high-security custody, which he's indicated is
what he wants. He has said he will not cooperate with any further
psychiatric reviews. It appears he recognises that young women in
the community are safer if he stays in custody, even if he refuses to
say so explicitly. Lloyd has been kept inside by virtue of a law that
allows for the indefinite detention of serious sexual offenders who
continue to present a high risk of reoffending. However, unfortunately for his victims, recognition of this risk and application of the
appropriate legislation did not come soon enough to protect them.
Indeed, it will remain rare for indefinite detention to be applied
after a first offence, falling short of an exceptional murder. Society
will never be capable of preventing all sadistic serial offending. But
hopefully we can get better at reducing reoffending by recognising
the signs of psychopathic sadism at an earlier stage in the offender's
violent life.

MANY PATHS TO MURDER, MANY VICTIMS

The case studies I have presented in this book illustrate the fact that murder is the culmination of many influences and can be committed by many types of people. Some of these people have trauma in their background that might make it less than totally surprising that they could become violent under particular life stressors. Experiences of emotional deprivation, physical abuse or sexual violation can leave deep scars, the buried fear and rage bursting to the surface later in life and leaving a victim lying dead, either a former abuser or a random surrogate who has taken the blame.

Others who become serial rapists and murderers can be driven by powerful deviant sexual drives, the origins of which are not always explicable. When those drives and orientations are linked with psychopathic personality traits that render the person unfeeling towards others, the mix is potentially deadly. If that individual has had experiences in their past that cause them to be enraged with others, perhaps women in particular, the combination of a strong sexual drive and a need to hurt or humiliate can produce the serial sadistic offender. These people can be the most troubling to assess, and the most dangerous if left to their own devices in the community.

But perhaps for the average reader of these case studies, the most disturbing examples will be those people who come from unremarkable backgrounds, with no previous trauma and no criminal history, people who have led stable and productive lives before they are derailed by extraordinary events or the onset of a psychotic illness that takes away their rationality. There can be a realisation that 'There but for the grace of God go I'. You may well be left wondering if you, or someone close to you, could become a murderer.

From a basic statistical standpoint, this is highly unlikely. But in a sense, any one of us could become a murderer. Given the right combination of circumstances or symptoms, our killer instinct could be released. It is an awareness of, and attention to, any relevant risk factors in ourselves and those we know best that will help us avoid becoming a statistic.

Many people in society tend to link murder to mental illness. This is understandable, but the fact is that the majority of murders are not the result of mental illness. Far more likely are motivations such as drug disputes, vengeance, or strong human emotions such as jealous rage or displaced male pride. Alcohol or drug intoxication is a very common factor in triggering violence that may become murder. Being drunk or stoned can have a grave effect on the brain's ability to make normal judgements and rational decisions.

Mental health authorities are generally at pains to stress that violence resulting from mental illness is uncommon, that most of the people with those illnesses will not be harmfully aggressive. Stigma against the mentally ill is significant, and it is therefore seen as important to educate the general public about this low risk of violence in order to assist with the treatment and rehabilitation of mentally ill people in our society. But it is also important to be honest and up-front about the fact that psychosis can produce irrational violence, and at times result in murder. Particular types of illness are more likely to be associated with violence, and particular symptoms may point to a more heightened risk. The cases I have presented indicate those red flags. Paranoid types of psychosis;

delusions of persecution; voices commanding the person to kill; psychotic depression with feelings of hopelessness and despair; drug-induced psychoses with the inclusion of family members in paranoid delusions—these are all among the factors that raise the potential for murderous violence.

Becoming more aware of those higher-risk patients, and being more proactive in getting them effective treatment, will reduce the chances of them acting on their irrational beliefs, with possibly tragic results. The cases of psychosis that I have described indicate that those murders arose from those illnesses and, retrospectively, it is possible to see how different treatment, given earlier, might have been preventive. But the cases also indicate the considerable difficulties for families and professionals in recognising the developing risk and predicting the potential disastrous consequences in order to prevent them.

While there are many paths to murder, there are also many more victims than the person who ends up being killed. That deceased person is the primary victim, having lost their life. But there are usually many secondary victims. Close family will grieve the loss of their loved one, and their lives will usually never be the same again. They will suffer the trauma of what they have seen or heard in regard to the killing. They may develop post-traumatic stress disorder or some other medical complication. Children may be left parentless, with all the long-term issues that can cause. A family that has experienced a murder in its midst, even when those people bear no responsibility for the event, can feel the stigma of what has occurred for the rest of their lives.

In many cases, the family members of the murderer are secondary victims as well, feeling guilt and remorse on behalf of the murderer, even if they have no remorse themselves. Any loyalty to the murderer will create very conflicted feelings. These people will probably be stigmatised too, and their lives irrevocably changed.

Neighbours or other witnesses less directly connected to the murder may also suffer trauma. The emergency workers and police attending the scene of the crime will need to confront a shocking sight and deal with distressed people. Even members of the general public can feel unsettled by a murder in their community. This is the ripple effect of a very violent event.

It must not be forgotten that the person who carries out the murder can also be a victim. This is most obvious when the crime has been the result of a serious mental illness which has turned a previously well and functional person into an irrational killer. The killer will spend years in hospital, and a lifetime on a forensic order. Once they recover from their illness, they will have to confront the reality of what they did and grieve for the victim, who was very likely a close family member. They may never be able to resume close ties with their children or other loved ones. They will always bear the shame of having been a killer, even though the illness that prompted it was not of their making, and they will likely bear a great burden of guilt, even though the illness was not their fault. They will likely not experience ready acceptance by a community that does not understand and fears being too close to such awful events. Nor should they expect politicians to be supportive. There are no votes in murder, even when it is the tragic result of a mental illness—tough talk and punitive policies are more likely to find favour. The media is rarely empathetic, often referring to the ill offender in lurid terms such as 'crazed killer'.

In the case of non-psychotic murderers, it is possible to feel some empathy towards those whose past life experiences and stressful events led them to kill. They will be incarcerated for a very long time and their future will be bleak. Fortunately, for some, the prison system may be reasonably kind. They may receive education and treatment they might otherwise have never had, and the parole system may eventually recognise that they have worked hard to rehabilitate themselves. They may then get a second chance at a life in the community. Some will succeed in salvaging a life for themselves and become good citizens.

But there are some murderers for whom it seems impossible to feel any empathy, or mercy. Psychiatrists do not think in terms of people being evil, but there are some killers for whom little hope is held. They are incapable of empathy for others. They are so self-centred and narcissistic that they are incapable of rehabilitation. They feel no remorse for their offences, and perhaps live for the day when they can rape and kill again. If they are victims of something in their make-up or background that has made them a killer, the precise reasons are beyond our ability to understand: genetics have something to do with it; there is some evidence that their brains may develop differently; many have a history of severe early deprivation or abuse. But they are beyond treatment or redemption. While they are in prison, the outside community is protected from them, although the prison community is not necessarily as protected—murders still occur inside. For these people, the correctional system bears the burden of keeping the community safe, and the community pays the costs. In that sense, in a small way, we are all their victims.

This is the sombre reality of murder. For those closely involved, the trauma is real, adjustment is difficult, forgetting is impossible. Yet, for the rest of us, murder is all the rage. We devour our murder mystery novels. We relax in front of our televisions, watching the village folk of country England killing two or three of their number every week, or revelling in the seamy underbelly killings in major cities around the world. Fictional murder provides the most common plot, but true crime also has a strong following. Historical murders are fascinating, the more gruesome the better. Unsolved cold cases are an interesting challenge. Stories about murders in our own community take up a lot of newspaper inches and get much attention in tea break or dinner party conversations.

This is murder at arm's-length, real enough to scare or fascinate, mostly not enough to do us damage. In most cases the good people win—the murderer is caught and justice is served. We probably feel uncomfortable when there is no resolution or if the bad person wins. This may be a clue as to why we are so enamoured of murder as entertainment. Perhaps it provides a way for us to deal with deep fears or repressed anger within ourselves, or even a safe way to entertain aggressive fantasies, our inner killer instinct, knowing that in the end we haven't actually done any harm. Resolution and a return to equilibrium are important. Seeing justice done can provide inner reassurance. This play therapy of murder entertainment with a happily resolved ending is just what we need to help us relax. Better not to overthink the reasons why it works so well for us.

I have been known to say to colleagues, lawyers or friends that 'I love a good murder!' That should not be misinterpreted. I do not love the violence and its dreadful consequences for all concerned. But I do relish the challenge of analysing a murder. I enjoy being able to put all my training, experience, acquired skills and accumulated knowledge into the task of answering the relevant diagnostic and legal questions. I approach the task with a degree of confidence that comes from years of practice.

Yet even now, some cases stretch my limits. They bother me and disturb my sleep. Human behaviour can still be perplexing and disturbing. I get frustrated when I am unable to find a way into an offender's inner mental life, most commonly in the case of sadistic killers.

To really understand a murderer, I feel I have to inhabit their mind. To do that, I have to gain access to it. I can use my interviewing skills, ask the right questions, pick up subtle clues, observe their emotional reactions, and try to gain their confidence and trust. I will get nowhere if I appear judgemental, disrespectful or easily shocked. I need to listen carefully and ask for clarification if I do not understand something. I will let them speak spontaneously if they are willing, but I will probe and persist even in the face of a reluctance to talk. If necessary, I will challenge inconsistencies in their account, or statements that don't match other evidence. The interview will be given as much time as it requires, often many hours, with appropriate breaks. Time, patience and persistence often pay off. As a forensic interviewer, I have the luxury of time to do the job. But where an offender is not ready to talk, unwilling to reveal the workings of their mind and the nature of their emotions, all my efforts may yield little of real value, and I will be left to rely on the external evidence and speculations to form an opinion.

My professional life is taken up with violence, sexual offending and murder. In my time off, I like to try to switch off and enjoy positive, amusing and uplifting things. At the cinema and in front of the television, I generally avoid horror and gratuitous violence. That feels a little too much like work, but oddly also not authentic enough. I do watch lighter murder mysteries and enjoy the settings, the subplots and the scenery, but I end up irritated by the scripted impossibility of identifying the killer. True crime shows can be enjoyable for me, but I tend to be a harsh critic of the methods employed or the standard of the analysis. True crime literature, when I get time to read, is often absorbing, and I am carried away by the writing skills of the better-known authors.

So, in a way, I do love a good murder, and in that regard I am like many people in society. But I do look at things to do with murder with a rather more critical and informed perspective than most. That is both a privilege and a burden.

APPENDIX—A GUIDE TO THE MEDICO-LEGAL MAZE

People who are not involved in legal matters, or who are unfamiliar with the medico-legal interface between medicine and the law, find it difficult to comprehend how an offender progresses through the legal processes. It is even more complex when there are questions about mental illness defences or fitness to plead and stand trial. The reporting of legal matters in the media not uncommonly reflects such a lack of understanding. This guide will hopefully assist in understanding the processes.

The arrest and charge
When a killing occurs, the first task for police is to gather evidence and catch the suspect. In the majority of cases the killer will be identified quickly, but even then, much evidence will be accumulated to ensure a future conviction. Sometimes it takes a long time to identify the killer. DNA evidence has been revolutionary in ensuring the right person is convicted, or other persons of interest are eliminated.

First stage of assessment
Once an offender is arrested, an initial assessment should occur to exclude the presence of any mental health issues. The police will interview the defendant before a charge is laid, and if they notice any obvious signs of mental illness they will probably involve the duty medical officer.

Screening for intoxicants
Hopefully, a sample of urine or blood will be collected very soon after the person's arrest to clarify the role of any intoxication in the offending. Unfortunately, this is not necessarily as high on the list of priorities for the police as it is for forensic clinicians, perhaps because the detection of drugs or alcohol in the system may invalidate a

police interview. For the forensic service, knowing about levels of drugs and alcohol may be crucial in making later assessments of the presence or absence of a mental health defence.

Second stage of assessment

Any obvious evidence of psychosis or disturbed behaviour in the prison cell will lead to a more intense mental health assessment, at first by a forensic clinician (usually a nurse or a psychologist) and then often by a forensic psychiatrist. In Queensland, it is routine for the forensic psychiatry service to seek an assessment of every prisoner newly charged with murder. However, that can only be done with the defendant's consent, and this may be withheld, particularly if a lawyer is involved at this early stage.

Magistrates Court appearance

As soon as possible after their arrest, the defendant will appear in the Magistrates Court for a preliminary hearing. If they don't have their own lawyer, a duty lawyer will represent them. The main issues at that stage will be whether there is any serious mental illness that requires the defendant to be transferred to hospital, and failing that, whether they can be granted bail into the community pending trial. Bail for a murder charge can only be granted by the Supreme Court. Mental health concerns will be communicated to the magistrate by the forensic psychiatry service. If required, the defendant could be sent to a mental health unit for treatment at this early stage.

Bail or remand in custody

Most people charged with murder will not be granted bail quickly. After a few days or a week in the watchhouse, the defendant will be sent to a remand section of a prison set aside for the detention of prisoners awaiting trial.

Third stage of assessment

While on remand, the defendant can be further assessed by medical staff and the prison mental health service if required. They can receive visits from their lawyer to work on what the defence, if any, will be.

Waiting for trial

For the majority of people charged with murder, there will be no further involvement with forensic psychiatry services. There will be a prolonged wait for a trial, partly because courts are busy, but also because the prosecution and defence will need time to assemble all the evidence.

The committal hearing

In time, a committal hearing will be held in the Magistrates Court. The prosecution will put the evidence forward and the magistrate will determine whether there is a sufficiently cogent case to put before a jury. When this is the finding, an indictment will be presented in the Supreme Court, where serious matters such as murder are tried. The case will be mentioned in court for case management, and if it is not referred to the Mental Health Court, it will be given a trial listing before a judge and jury; or, if it becomes a matter simply for sentence, there will be a sentencing hearing.

The Mental Health Court

In Queensland, there is a distinct section of the Supreme Court called the Mental Health Court (MHC), which determines matters of psychiatric defence and fitness for trial. In this respect, the processes diverge from those in other jurisdictions.

Referral to the Mental Health Court

If there are questions of mental illness that might produce a defence of unsoundness of mind or unfitness for trial, the defendant will be referred to the MHC by their lawyer, the prosecution, a magistrate, or the chief psychiatrist in the Health Department. Once a referral is made, the proceedings in other courts are suspended while the MHC makes its determination.

Fourth stage of assessment

During this entire process, from the time of arrest, if it is clear that the defendant is very unwell, they will most likely be transferred to a secure hospital for treatment while awaiting trial, and the referral to the MHC will occur there. In preparation for the MHC trial, psychiatric assessments and reports will be prepared at the request of lawyers and the MHC itself. In murder trials in the MHC, at least three such reports are usually given.

The Mental Health Court: structure and functions

The Supreme Court judge who comprises the MHC is assisted by two psychiatrists who sit on the bench with the judge and provide advice to the court as to how it should assess the evidence it receives on clinical issues. Such a referral will only be processed in the MHC if there is no disputing of the facts. The defendant has to accept the fact of the killing and any requisite intention, but the MHC will have the task of deciding whether there is a defence of unsoundness of mind or diminished responsibility, and rule on fitness for trial.

The processes in the MHC differ from those in a normal trial, with there being an inquisitorial approach rather than the adversarial style of other courts. The level of proof required is at the level of the balance of probabilities rather than beyond reasonable doubt, as would apply in a disputed murder trial. The fact that the MHC orders independent reports, and that expert witnesses can be questioned by the assisting psychiatrists during the trial, means that the standard of evidence must be high.

Assuming, then, that the defendant does not dispute the facts of the killing, proceedings will continue and both sides will present to the MHC all the evidence relating to mental capacity.

Presumption of sanity

In this jurisdiction, there is a presumption that the defendant was sane or of sound mind at the time of the murder. To establish a defence of unsoundness of mind, the MHC will have to be persuaded on all the evidence that, at the time of the killing, the defendant was suffering from a mental illness sufficient to completely deprive them of one or more of three capacities.

The three capacities

The three capacities relevant to the insanity defence concern a person's ability to:

1. know what they were doing
2. know that they ought not to do it (know it was wrong)
3. control their actions.

Impairment versus deprivation of liberties

Impairment of these capacities is insufficient for unsoundness of mind. Complete deprivation of at least one capacity is needed, in the absence of intoxication with alcohol or drugs. If the finding is of unsoundness of mind, that means that the person is regarded by law as not criminally responsible for the killing, and thereafter they are managed as a psychiatric patient rather than a prisoner. This means they will be placed on a forensic order under the *Mental Health Act* and be transferred from prison to a secure psychiatric hospital.

Forensic order

A forensic order is a special form of involuntary treatment order. It is applied in cases of serious offending after the court makes a finding of unsoundness, or unfitness for trial. It can only be removed by the Mental Health Review Tribunal (MHRT), which overseas involuntary psychiatric treatment in this system. A patient who has committed a murder will generally spend years in hospital and will only be allowed leave to be treated in the community once they are sufficiently well or in remission, and once the risk of any reoffending has been minimised. They will be under the forensic order, in most cases, for the rest of their life.

Diminished responsibility

The MHC has the other option of finding diminished responsibility in cases where there has been a killing. If the defendant is found to not have a defence of unsoundness of mind, they may neverthe-less be found to be suffering from an 'abnormality of mind', such as a mental illness, intellectual handicap or brain damage, sufficient to cause substantial impairment of the same three capacities as for unsoundness. This impairment is not total deprivation, as for unsoundness, but it is nevertheless sufficient to reduce the respon-sibility of the person for their actions.

From murder to manslaughter

A finding of diminished responsibility has the effect of reducing the charge from one of murder to one of manslaughter. That lesser charge does not carry the sentence of mandatory life imprisonment that follows a murder conviction. Presuming the defendant is fit for trial, the finding will mean that the case moves from the MHC to the mainstream Supreme Court, usually for sentencing. That court has much more flexibility in sentencing for manslaughter and can impose anything from a non-custodial sentence to life in prison. In countries that prescribe the death sentence for murder, reducing a charge from murder to manslaughter is obviously of even more significance.

Temporarily unfit for trial

If the MHC determines that the defendant was not mentally unsound at the time of the killing, it then has the task of determin-ing fitness for trial. If the person is fit for trial, the order will be for the matter to proceed according to law, which means that the trial returns to the mainstream Supreme Court before a jury. If the MHC determines that the defendant is unfit for trial on a temporary basis, they will be placed on a forensic order and sent to a secure hospital for treatment until the MHRT finds them fit, at which time they will return to the remand prison and face their trial.

Permanently unfit for trial

Occasionally, a defendant who has committed a murder will be found by the MHC to be permanently unfit for trial. This could occur, for example, if the defendant is suffering from a progressive dementia or has acquired a severe brain injury. In that case, the MHC has the option not to make a forensic order, if it were seen to have no value in ensuring treatment of the defendant or protecting the public.

Appeals from the Mental Health Court

A party dissatisfied with a decision of the MHC can appeal to the Court of Appeal.

The Supreme Court

If there is no referral to the MHC and the defendant is pleading not guilty, the trial progresses from the committal stage to the Supreme Court for a jury to determine guilt or innocence and, if the finding is guilt, for the judge to pass sentence. In jurisdictions other than Queensland, all the issues relating to mental illness defences and fitness for trial, along with the basic issue of guilt or innocence regarding the killing, will be determined by the judge or jury in the equivalent of the Supreme Court.

Trial

If a defendant does not wish to accept the finding of the MHC denying them a defence of unsoundness of mind or a partial defence of diminished responsibility, they have the option of taking the matter to a trial in the mainstream Supreme Court to try their luck with a jury. In practice, that occurs only rarely.

Fitness to plead and fitness for trial

At trial, the defendant is required to plead guilty or not guilty—to be fit to plead, they must understand the meaning of those terms. Fitness for trial, however, means more than just fitness to plead. The defendant will need to be able to instruct their lawyer, meaning they need to be able to give their account of what happened and their role in the alleged events. They will need to have a basic understanding of how a court functions and the roles of the various entities in court. Many first-time offenders will have gleaned their knowledge of these matters from watching courtroom trials on TV or in movies. If they are not sure about what will go on, they need to have the capacity to be educated by their lawyer.

The defendant needs to know that they can challenge potential jurors whom they may see as biased against them for some reason. They must understand the role of the jury in determining guilt or innocence. They also need to be aware of the role played by the prosecution and defence barristers. They need to know that the judge will guide the court proceedings and ultimately hand down the sentence if the jury finds the person guilty.

A common-sense approach to the question of fitness for trial means that a person does not need to have a sophisticated understanding of all these things, simply a reasonable ability to understand and participate with the appropriate assistance of their lawyer, who is there to act on their behalf and speak for them in court.

In addition to all of this, there is the question of whether the defendant is fit enough to withstand the rigours of a trial without suffering severe damage to their mental health. Can they follow proceedings to a reasonable extent, if necessary with the assistance of their lawyer? Or are they too intellectually handicapped, too depressed or too hampered by psychosis to properly attend to what is going on? Will the stress of court or the giving of evidence be enough to severely worsen an already significant illness? Are they able to comprehend sufficiently to challenge, if necessary, the evidence that other witnesses may give?

The task for the jury

The task for a jury hearing a murder trial can be onerous and complex. The trial may last for weeks, many witnesses may give evidence and be cross-examined, and the medical evidence may be hard to understand for a layperson unfamiliar with technical terms and medical jargon. Experts for either side may provide conflicting opinions that are difficult to reconcile. The legal technicalities and definitions are often obtuse to non-lawyers. The evidence is also quite likely to be explicit and potentially traumatic, taking the jurors to places beyond their normal life experience and definitely out of their comfort zone. The secret and often prolonged jury room deliberations will also probably be difficult. The judge will try to assist the jury with a clear summing up and will guide them in making sense of the processes and the requirements of the court. But all that can take its toll and it is not a task most people would relish, nor one that they would want to do more than once.

The sentence

Once there is a guilty verdict, whether for murder or manslaughter, the judge will pass sentence. In Queensland, a murder conviction means a mandatory life sentence. For many murderers, eligibility for parole will begin after fifteen years, unless the sentencing judge has set a longer period. It is then up to the Parole Board to decide if the offender is sufficiently rehabilitated to mitigate the risk and allow release into the community on parole. A murderer remains on parole for the rest of their life and is subject to the supervision of the Probation and Parole Office.

The role of the media

It is important for the media to report on serious cases of violence and killing. Unfortunately, in cases where a defendant successfully raises a psychiatric defence, the media reporting will sometimes be inaccurate. The description of the defendant may contribute to the stigmatising of a mentally ill person. It will often be reported that the defendant was found unfit for trial, when in fact they were found to be of unsound mind at the time of the killing. The media report may imply that in some way the killer has 'got off' and avoided punishment, with a failure on the part of the journalist to recognise that in fact the defendant has been found to be so seriously unwell that they were not criminally responsible for their actions, and that they now face years of hospital treatment and a lifetime of careful monitoring on a forensic order. There is often a failure to understand that the outcome is one that means not only that the patient will be treated, but that the community will be kept safer than if the killer had gone to prison, not treated, and were in time released on parole still suffering from a potentially dangerous psychotic condition.

ACKNOWLEDGEMENTS

I started this book as a novice writer, having to learn how to adapt my writing from that appropriate for a formal medico-legal report to a more narrative style for general readers. I am very grateful for all the help I have received with this project.

I was most fortunate when my agent, Margaret Kennedy, agreed to take me on as an unproven prospect. She was immensely helpful in advising how to structure the book and when to leave things out. Her ideas and suggestions prompted me to incorporate the unifying themes that meld theoretical notions with case examples. Her assistance with the submissions to publishers was invaluable.

Along the way, friends, family and colleagues in psychiatry and the law have encouraged and supported me. Particular thanks go to Dr Julian Davis, Prof. Fiona Judd, Dr June Donsworth, Prof. Alastair Blanshard, Prof. Gordon Parker, Justice Margaret McMurdo AC, Daryl Warren and Julie Warren, and my sister, Joy Grant Hicks. Others who wish to remain anonymous know who they are and I thank them.

My two children and their spouses are getting used to the idea that I am now a true crime author. They have urged me on and are anxious to read the result of my efforts. My grandchildren, however, have been told that they must wait until they are eighteen before they will be allowed to have a read. My partner, David Hill, has been a great support and immensely patient.

I was extremely pleased and gratified when Melbourne University Publishing took on this project. They seemed as excited as me! I feel I have had a dream run at my first attempt. The team under Sally Heath—Emma Rusher and Georgie MacRae in publicity, Paul Smitz as copyeditor and Cathryn Lea Smith, senior editor—have been reassuring, enthusiastic and professional. I have learned a lot from them and continue to do so. I look forward to the path ahead with their guidance and support.

INDEX

Wilson, Colin
  develops melanoma 95–6
  early life 96–7
  kills mother 91–105
  plans suicide 93–4
Wilson, Ida, killed by son 91–105
Wilson, Jean 97–8, 101–2
witchcraft 6
Wolston Park mental hospital 106
Worldwide Church of God 52–3
wrongfulness, legal vs moral 72